SANDHILLS KID

IN THE CITY

1927 - 1938

Sandhills Kid
in the City
1927 - 1938

Billie Lee Snyder Thornburg

THE OLD HUNDRED AND ONE PRESS
North Platte , Nebraska

Published by the Old 101 Press
2220 Leota Street
North Platte, NE 69101

Printed in the United States of America

Cover Design by Diane Solomon
Book Design by Kai Crozer
Edited by Ann Milton

Library of Congress Control Number: 2004109785
Thornburg, Billie Lee Snyder
Sandhills Kid in the City: 1927 - 1938 / by Billie Lee Snyder Thornburg
p.cm
Summary: A humorous and historical account of a young girl who moved from the Sandhills of Nebraska to go to high school in Salem, Oregon and then back to North Platte, Nebraska to teach dancing lessons. This memoir takes place during the years 1927 to 1938.
ISBN 0-9721613-7-6

Introduction

The six Snyders whom you met in *Bertie and Me* and *Bertie and Me and Miles Too* found living in Salem, Oregon far different than living in the Sandhills of Nebraska. It was thrilling, exciting and painful. The family toughed it out until Bertie and Billie finished four years of high school and graduated. As soon as school was out, the family headed back to Nebraska and spent the rest of their lives in McPherson and Lincoln Counties where they belonged. All, that is, except Bertie and Billie who at 90 and 92 are still living their lives—but they haven't any long trips planned.

*The cover was created from this
photo of Billie demonstrating
her flexibility at age eleven.*

Chapter One

THE FAMILY ARRIVES IN OREGON

It was the summer of the year 1927. My older sister Nellie was twenty-two, my brother Miles was twenty, I was fifteen and my little sister Bertie was thirteen. It was the last day of our two-month long trip from our ranch in the Sandhills of Nebraska to the shores of the Pacific coast in Oregon. We were to live in Salem for the next four years while the folks leased our ranch in Nebraska and sent Bertie and me to high school in Oregon.

When I had finished grade school Dad had said, "If you wait until Bertie graduates from eighth grade before you go to high school, I'll take you all out and show you there's something in this world besides the Sandhills." Secretly I think Dad was looking for better ranch country. The Sandhills were getting too fenced in for him. I also think Mama was afraid to send me to town to go to high school by myself.

Our family of six had spent the night camped in tents south of Portland and as close to the Pacific Ocean as we could get. In the morning we all stood and stared at the ocean we had read so much about. Finally to break the silence I said, "Hmmm, that's not so much." The folks all laughed and kidded me for years about how I refused to show I was impressed by the ocean.

The status in the Snyder family was: Dad and Mama were still bosses over all of us; Nellie was the GREAT BRAIN and we all looked up to her; Miles was the

The road along the Oregon coast in the 1920s. You had to be careful.

strong, quiet one who kept everything in working order; and then there were Bertie and me who were still trying to find our places in the big world around us.

We called Nellie the GREAT BRAIN because she knew many words and the meaning of them all—even how to spell them. I remember hearing her say, "I like words. I like the way they feel when they roll off my tongue." (Sometimes it seemed to me she tried to roll them all off in one conversation. Years later when Nellie was paid to give talks I thought, *Gee Whiz, there were times I would have paid her not to talk.* I'm sure the folks would have paid her to keep quiet at times, too, if they had only thought of it.) Don't get me wrong, the whole family loved Nellie and we all took advantage of her GREAT BRAIN whenever the need arose. I never looked a word up in the dictionary if Nellie was in yelling distance.

Nellie remembered all she read or heard. Sometimes she remembered big, but we never called it exaggeration. Her stories were always interesting. She wrote thirteen books in her lifetime and anyone who interviewed her walked away with more than he/she came after, thinking all the while, *What a great person to talk to.*

I fully expected to have a great brain like Nellie's when I grew up. It never happened.

Right now I'm a little ashamed to think of the times in junior high school English when I was supposed to write a report on a classic. Instead of reading the book, I would have Nellie tell me the story and write my report from that.

Nellie the Great Brain.

I was with Nellie when she died, January 16, 1992. The instant she took her last breath the thought went through my head that all the history stored in her brain was gone forever. They say you can't take money with you when you die but you do take everything in your brain.

Miles didn't use any more words than necessary, but his eyes, his slow, one-sided grin and his facial expressions told more than words. He noticed and remembered everything that went on around him. He was very much missed when a couple of years down the road he joined the Army and was gone from home for two years.

Then there were Bertie and me. I told about us in the two books *Bertie and Me* and *Bertie and Me and Miles Too*. In this book we are country kids learning to live in the big city.

We packed up our camping gear, bedrolls and the three tents we had lived in for weeks, and I do mean weeks. We had spent almost a month in Yellowstone alone. We had broken camp so many times it did not take long, even going slow. We soon had everything in place in our 1926 Ford touring car and in the old 1920 Ford made into a version of a pickup. We were to arrive at Aunt Alice's two miles north of Salem that afternoon. None of us had ever seen Aunt Alice or Uncle Gene, but they were relatives and we were anxious to meet them.

We headed from our beautiful campsite by the ocean down a black, two-lane, paved road to Salem. There was only room for two cars, one going each way at the same time. I don't remember what the speed limit was or if there was one. There was no stripe painted down the center to make the drivers stay on their own side of the road. It was the longest strip of paving we had seen on our entire trip and we enjoyed the drive very much.

There were hundreds of beautiful, tall trees on both sides of the road. If there were nothing else taking up the space there would be trees. Occasionally we would see a little house in the trees. We thought the trees were wonderful, like tall Christmas trees, but we felt penned in. A person couldn't see very far. Back home, no matter where we were, we could see until the sky touched the ground.

As we got farther from Portland and nearer to Salem, we saw more and more fruit farms. Uncle Gene and Aunt Alice owned a small berry farm. They were expecting us when our two cars pulled up in front of their old, two-story, white house.

The only snow storm we had while in Salem. Nellie and friend.

It was the middle of the afternoon. We had no doubt stopped as usual along the side of the road to eat our dinner, as we had done all across the country when we weren't camped for a few days at a nice spot. As we traveled, our dinners were crackers with either sharp cheese or sardines, eaten by the side of the road. We drank water from a jug that we carried in one of the cars. In those days you couldn't stop at a service station, go in and drink cold water from a fountain. And we didn't waste money on pop. We carried water with us as I imagine many people did.

Dad usually had a story to tell about the part of the country we were going through. I remember one noon very clearly. We were in sagebrush country in Wyoming and Dad saw a good place to pull off to the side of the road to "noon" as he called it. He made it very clear we were all to watch out carefully for ticks, especially Bertie and me if we went walking out in the sagebrush. He said if one of those ticks bit us, it could make us very sick and we might even die. Dad said he had been bitten by a Wyoming tick once and almost died. He went on and told us of an old cowboy he knew who did die from tick fever.

Bertie and I liked to wander around and see what things were like but we didn't take a look around after dinner that day. We were in a hurry to get out of that place.

Aunt Alice had room for all of us and made us feel she had been waiting all her life for us to come to visit her. We three girls had a large upstairs room with two beds. We looked forward to sleeping in a bed in a house instead of in a bedroll outdoors.

The first night we went up to bed at the same time as we usually did. Nellie pulled the chain that turned off the overhead light bulb. The room seemed so dark—it even seemed as though there wasn't enough air to take a good breath. None of us could go to sleep.

First Nellie got up and went to the window. (The windows did not have screens on them. There were no flies or mosquitoes.) Nellie stood there leaning against the windowsill, putting her head out as far as it would go and looking up at the sky. Soon Bertie and I joined her. It felt wonderful to see the sky and the stars. It was also easier to breathe. We all spent the first part of that night sticking our heads out the open window. It took several nights for us to break ourselves into sleeping in a room once more.

Just now as I was writing about leaning out the window without screens, I got a flashback to how it was on the ranch. During the summertime we had flies aplenty. Our big ranch kitchen had two outside doors, one on the north towards the barn and one on the south leading to the backyard, the garden and the lake below. All our coming and going seemed to be through that north door. That was the one with all the flies around it even though we went in and out as fast as possible. (I can still hear Mama yelling at us kids, "DON'T HOLD THAT DOOR OPEN!" and the guilty party quickly finishing going in or out.)

We had those sticky, spiral things hanging around and used the fly swatters plenty. The flies still got ahead of us in that big kitchen. There were many evenings Mama would tell Bertie and me to each grab a dishtowel and help her shoo the flies out. That's what we did, each swinging her dishtowel and saying, "Shoo," while we headed the flies toward an agreed upon door. When the time was just right, the person closest to the screen door quickly pushed it open and held it while the other two shooed the herd of flies out. The "door opener" closed the door in a hurry. Mama would look the room over and sometimes find that we hadn't gotten most of the flies. Then we had to do it all over again.

In Salem we didn't even need screens on the doors or windows. No flies, no cow chips, what could be better?

Chapter Two

PICKING FRUIT

Uncle Gene and Aunt Alice both were short, round and very jolly. They liked kids the ages of Bertie and me. In fact, they were raising a grandson, Mike. Mike's age was between Bertie and me. He livened things up for us.

Mike was a big tease and was always dreaming up ways to let us know he was around. One night we three girls went up to our room to go to bed. Bertie reached up and pulled the chain to turn the overhead light on. The light came on but went off again right away. This happened a few times and then we noticed a string leading from the light chain going straight to the open window. We went over and looked out the window and there was Mike holding the other end of the string and giggling up a quiet storm.

Uncle Gene and Aunt Alice told us about all the fruit there was for us kids to pick. The best part was we would get paid for picking it. None of us had gotten money for working on the ranch as kids, except the time Dad gave me five dollars at the end of haying the first year I drove stacker team. I was six years old. I bought two doll buggies with my five dollars—one for Bertie and one for myself. I always felt Dad didn't like what I spent the money for since he never paid me again.

Uncle Gene told us that in the spring and early summer there were berries: strawberries, raspberries (red and black), and cherries (Bing and Royal Annes). Two berries we had never heard of were black caps and red caps. They were delicious but the stickers on the vines made them hard to pick. We didn't care. We got money for the picking.

Then came prunes, plums, apples, pears and hops. It was enough to keep a kid busy all summer. I had no idea there was a place like this.

The berry season was over by the time we arrived at Aunt Alice's so our first job was picking prunes. That was fun. We didn't even have to climb the trees to get to the fruit. We had tall ladders with a place on top of the ladder to set the bucket. We picked the bucket full of fruit, climbed down the ladder and took the bucket to the scales where the fruit was weighed and we were given credit. We worked in the shade. It sure beat picking up cow chips out in the pasture on a hot, windy afternoon on the ranch back in Nebraska.

Nellie and Harry Yost (Nellie's husband) the way we looked picking choke cherries in Nebraska.

The owners of the orchard were Swiss brothers and sisters. They worked with the rest of the pickers. They yodeled as soon as they got on their ladders and started picking. We had never heard yodeling before. It was beautiful being out in the open and hearing the yodeling echoing from all different directions. It sounded better than hearing old cows bawling while we picked up cow chips. I could imitate an old cow bawling, but I tried to yodel and couldn't do it. There are two things I've always wanted to be able to do, one is to yodel and the other is to wiggle my ears. I gave up yodeling, but I'm still trying to wiggle my ears.

I remember what I bought with my first fruit-picking money—a good jackknife with more than just two blades and a leather belt with a pretty buckle. I'd wanted a good jackknife for years. I had a kid jackknife when I was back on the ranch. It was big with two very dull blades and it had a chain that fastened it into my overall pocket so I wouldn't lose it. I secretly wanted a jackknife like Miles had and now I had it. I don't remember ever using it.

I don't know why I wanted a leather belt. Girls didn't wear anything that required a leather belt back then. That was the year 1927, during the flapper craze. Girls wore belts all right, but they were worn riding just above the hips and they were not leather.

Chapter Three

Our New Home

Aunt Alice lived on a graveled side road about one-eighth of a mile from the paved road that we came down from Portland on. There was an auto camp built along the black road before you turned into Aunt Alice's. The auto camp was for sale. Dad bought it.

An old-fashioned, two-story house with a green lawn all around it came with the auto camp. I say the house was old-fashioned, but it was uptown to us. There was an overhead electric light in every room. All you had to do was pull a string and the light bulb lit up. There was a sink in the kitchen that had a faucet. Cold water came out when you turned it on. No more pumping water.

There was a plowed field between the auto camp and Aunt Alice's big old house and her berry farm. After we moved in, we were living almost in Aunt Alice's front yard. Traipsing back and forth, we soon had a path going through that plowed field to Aunt Alice's. The next spring the farmer that owned the ground planted the whole field in tulips—red ones, yellow ones, white ones and pink ones—all in a design. That year we had a path through the tulips. And tip-toed through them.

One thing puzzled me about our new house. Could I jump off the porch? Although I was fifteen years old, I was still in the stage of seeing what was the highest thing I could jump off of. Back at the ranch, I was always climbing on things. I could jump off every building but the west edge of the slanting roofs of our barn and our house. The porch of our house on the ranch was a snap. The

The window I crawled out of and the porch roof I jumped off of.

house was built flat on the ground. I climbed the ladder to get on the house, but always jumped off the porch roof to get down. It was much faster. The rest of the family came down the ladder.

Our new house was built up off the ground with two steps going up to the porch. After eyeing that porch roof for a few days, I went up to our bedroom and crawled out the window (no screens), walked to the edge of the roof and jumped. I don't think anyone saw me. I hoped not. I was badly jarred. I felt that jump in every bone in my body. I still remember how hard my teeth went together.

That was my last jump. I was starting to grow out of being just a big kid, but I had a lot more bumps and hard knocks before turning into a young lady.

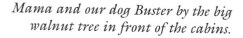

Mama and our dog Buster by the big walnut tree in front of the cabins.

When I was a little kid, I wanted to do all the things big people did. When I got big, I had a hard time letting go of the fun things kids did. I still have trouble living in the here-and-now. I'm always thinking ahead or thinking back though at ninety-one there isn't much to think forward to, so I seem to be thinking back more, as you see.

Mama and Dad sitting under the walnut tree.
I gained several pounds off that tree

Chapter Four

THE AUTO CAMP

The name of our new home was the Wenatchee Auto Camp. It had eleven cabins. There had been twelve but one burned down before Dad bought the camp. Eleven were plenty when it came to cleaning them after they had been stayed in all night. I heard Dad remark that he bought the auto camp because he taught his kids to work and he didn't want them to get out of the habit. We didn't.

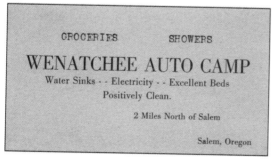
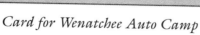

Card for Wenatchee Auto Camp

Wenatchee Auto Camp

The one-room cabins each had a carport. The cabins were about fourteen feet square with one door and a small window in the front. Inside there were two chairs, a small dining table, and one double-sized iron bedstead with bare bedsprings and mattress—no mattress cover. Each had a small, tin sink with a cold water faucet.

One of the cabins with Mama and Dad back by the toilet and showers.

Near the sink sat an iron wood-burning cook-stove. The little stove had two iron lids that were lifted off with an iron lid-lifter. There was space for a coffeepot and one skillet. Even during the summer, if the tenant wanted to cook a meal or make coffee, they had to light a fire. There were no hot plates or microwaves in those days.

Most tourists (I think they were called travelers in those days) if they were roughing it, carried their own bedding, even their pillows with them. They also carried all their dishes, pots, pans and eating utensils. People who didn't rough it stayed in hotels and ate in restaurants.

I remember one evening a car stopped and I went out to take care of the people in it. There was a real fancy lady in the car. I showed her a cabin. She liked it all right but said she would have to rent bed linens. I told her I would run in the house and see if we had any.

I told Mama that the lady wanted linens for the bed. Mama's mouth flew open as she drew in a big breath. We talked it over. We had lots of clean sheets and pillowcases but they certainly weren't made of linen. Mama gathered up the best pillows, sheets and pillowcases we had. I took those out. The woman was perfectly happy and we found out that sheets and pillowcases were called bed linens. We had much more to learn, as you'll soon see.

We charged two dollars a night for the cabins. The nights all the cabins were rented we had twenty-two dollars. I'd never seen so much money. I thought we

Miles in front of the filling station with the homemade pickup that Miles and I rode in to Oregon. The pickup was made from our 1920 Ford touring car.

were surely getting rich. Back on the ranch, our money was cattle. When something big had to be bought, the folks thought of it as how many steers it would take to buy it. Each fall Dad shipped cattle to Omaha. The stockyards paid him with a check. The check went in the bank. About the only cash we saw was the money we got for the cream and eggs we sold every two or three weeks and that always went for groceries. Twenty-two one-dollar bills in a stack were so pretty and far more than we ever received for the cream and eggs at one time. Here we were taking in money every day. I remember remarking to Mama about how much money we were making. She gave that laugh of hers that let me know it wasn't that way at all. Years later, I caught on. We made more money on the ranch. That big check in the fall made a big difference.

The auto camp had another little building right next to the black road. It had one gasoline pump in front. There was space for a car to pull off the road and park beside the pump.

We were very proud of that pump and we got a kick out of operating it. It had a glass top marked off in gallons. To fill the top with gas, we pushed the handle on the side of the pump back and forth. Then we unscrewed the gas tank cap on the car, put the nozzle in the hole and held the lever on the pump handle of the nozzle tight so the gas ran into the tank. The glass top was much higher than the hose and nozzle; gravity brought the gas down. We all felt important putting gas in the tank.

I think the glass tube held ten gallons of gas. The local people never put ten gallons in the gas tank at once. Only the travelers filled their tanks. When a car drove in for gas, we raced to see who could get there first to wait on them. That is, we raced at first. After a while it seemed more like work.

Other services we offered were an oil check, air for the tires and water for the radiator. We felt like quite the operators and the customers didn't let on if they noticed we were a little green at the job.

We also sold cigarettes: Lucky Strikes, Chesterfields and Camels. Those were the only brands on the market. None of us smoked except Dad. He smoked a pipe so we were not hard on the stock of cigarettes. The candy bars we sold were a different story. I started gaining weight at that time. I don't remember the price of the gas or the cigarettes. I sure remember those big Almond Hershey bars were only five cents. And they were huge and lumpy with nuts and not a word on the wrapper as to how many calories in each bar. I didn't know or care what a calorie was at that time. I watch them now though.

Nellie at the Wenatchee Auto Camp gas pump tending the service station.

The only service the traveler needed besides water was a little love, which Nellie is giving.

Back to the cabins. Each morning after the camper moved out, the cabin had to be cleaned and readied for a new tenant that night. No one liked that job. Dad knew what he was doing when he bought the Wenatchee Auto Court so his kids wouldn't forget how to work.

If the campers cooked their suppers and/or breakfasts, there would be coffee grounds in the sink and the stove would be dirty. We always had to get a pan of hot, soapy water from our house to clean the sink and the stove. The little stove burned wood so we had to clean the ashes out, bring in more wood, put a little paper and some twigs on top the wood and put heavier sticks on top of the twigs. The new camper only had to strike a match and light the paper and wait for the stove to heat up to start her cooking. Of course we filled the wood box by the stove with plenty of wood. After that we swept and mopped the floor and went on to the next cabin. About all you could say for that work was—it was better than picking up cow chips.

Toilets and showers, we had those, too. The toilets were the kind you flushed—quite a step up from the privy back on the ranch. They were in a long, narrow building, one side for men and one side for women. We all thought they were great even though they had to be cleaned every day during the season when travelers were stopping. There was a crude shower in each side of the building and hot water was supplied by one large gas-heated water tank.

The Auto Camp

A deep path led to this building that was located directly behind our house. All the campers used it as well as our family. Our family was used to going "out back" but I'm sure most of our campers had their own toilets in their houses back home. They were roughing it and probably told some good stories when they returned from their trips. The camper in Number One didn't have nearly as far to go to the toilet as the camper in Number Eleven.

If the camper went off and forgot something, the person who cleaned that cabin got to keep whatever it was. That was all Bertie and I got for cabin cleaning. The only good thing I remember being left was a very pretty, flashy, red and black sateen lounging robe. Bertie cleaned the cabin it was in that day and got to keep the robe. It just fit her. She was very proud of it and wore it for years.

The campers did not register in those early days. We didn't even take down their license plate numbers. That all came years later.

Bertie as a teenager in Salem at the Wenatchee Auto Camp.

Chapter Five

NELLIE AND THE BAPTISTS

Nellie joined the First Baptist Church. She took Bertie and me in with her. We had been baptized on the forehead by the Episcopal Bishop when we lived back on the ranch. Now we had to be baptized the other way. The Baptists had a big tank. The tank had a cover that was taken off when they baptized anyone. The preacher walked back and forth in front of it as he talked about sin and hellfire.

The big night came. All the people being baptized brought old clothes along to wear. We did, too. Preacher Payne was already standing in the middle of the tank when I walked down into the water. The water came up above my waist. Preacher Payne put one hand on my back and one hand tight over my mouth and nose. He tipped me back all at once and brought me right back up. The thought came to me as I came up, *I'm not an Episcopalian anymore, now I'm a Baptist*, but I didn't feel any different.

I took a fast look out into the congregation. It looked like there were a thousand people out there. I knew I must look terrible in those old, wet clothes.

The Sunday School and the Baptist Young Peoples Union meetings were the main part of our social life for the rest of our time in Salem.

Chapter Six

Nellie and the Jobs

Nellie wanted to get a job and have her own money again. She had done office work for Merricks General Store in Maxwell, Nebraska, for two years. She went to Millers Department Store in Salem, the biggest department store in town. They put her to work immediately.

Nellie tried twice to get me a weekend job in Millers Department Store. Neither time worked.

First the store needed someone to run the elevator on Saturdays. I can almost hear Nellie telling the boss, "I have a sister who can operate an elevator," knowing full well I'd never seen or been on one before the one in Millers Department Store.

The first Saturday I went to work knowing how much fun the job would be and it was. I had lots to learn but I even had a great time learning how to run the elevator.

The operator stood by the lever that was to the right side of the door. To make the elevator go up, the lever was pushed to the right. To make it go down, it was pushed to the left. The trick was to stop the car level with the floor. This was done by bringing the lever back to the upright position. If the elevator went too far, the person getting off would have to step down. If it didn't go far enough, the passengers had to step up. People didn't sue people in those days so it was all right if I got it just kind of close. I didn't even have to say, "Watch your step." They all knew they had better do that.

The elevator made a stop on the balcony. In fact, there were only four stops: the basement, first floor, the balcony and second floor. But on the balcony there was a little desk with pen, ink and writing paper.

I was getting better at the job, but one day no one seemed to want to ride the elevator. I got very bored. Then I had a happy thought. I would go up to that desk on the balcony and write a letter to a friend back home and tell her I was running an elevator. I would tell her how much more fun it was than milking cows.

I must have forgotten about the elevator. The first thing I knew someone came up to me and said, "A woman on the first floor rang for the elevator but it never showed up." That was the last day I ran the elevator for Millers Department Store.

Nellie did not give up easily. Later that winter Millers needed an extra sales-person in the Women's Ready to Wear Department down in the basement where the cheaper clothing was sold. This clerk would only work on Saturdays. Again, I can hear Nellie telling the store manager that she had a sister who was just right for that job. As the saying goes, "Nellie could talk the balls off a pool table."

While writing this I am reminded of a time when Nellie was visiting me. She got going on a subject I was not interested in. I listened for a long time but could tell she had a long ways to go yet. I suddenly got very busy making like I was cleaning house. I went from room to room as fast as I could, doing this and that. Nellie followed me from room to room, telling her story and not missing a word. (Nellie never forgot where she was in telling a story; when something interrupted her she would always go back to her story, picking it up at the exact spot where she was interrupted.)

Finally Nellie said in a very disgusted voice, "Billie, you are being very impolite by not listening to me."

I answered her by saying, "Nellie, you are the one being impolite by talking when you know I don't want to listen." We argued some more about which one of us was being impolite, then laughed it off. I never did hear the end of her story. If I could have her back for a day I would happily sit still and listen to anything she wanted to talk about.

Now back to the second time I was fired from Millers Department Store. As I remember there were three other clerks down there in the basement with the cheap clothes, too. I grabbed the first customer who came down the stairs. I did not want those girls to know I had never clerked in a store before.

Up to that point in my life, I not only had never clerked, I had never bought any clothing out of a store. Mama always made our clothing or ordered what she couldn't make from the Monkey Wards or the Sears Roebuck catalogs.

The customer was a small lady. I asked her what she wanted. She said she needed a new coat.

We were standing right by a coat rack, so I pulled a coat off the rack and put it on her. It was way too big. I looked around for the other clerks. I needed help! They were all standing to the side watching me, each with a grin on her face. The girls thought I knew how to clerk—or maybe they knew I had never clerked before and they were just waiting for me to fall flat on my face.

Finally one came over and bailed me out. Later she told me I should ask, "What size?" "What color?" "What kind?"

I only worked one day at that job. For some reason Millers Department Store forgot to call me to come back to work the next Saturday.

Chapter Seven

Nosy Neighbors

A couple named Will and Mrs. Powers lived just across the road from us in a house surrounded by tall, green trees. No sunshine ever reached it but they had a clear view of everything that went on at our place.

We seldom saw Will who was a school teacher in Salem. When we did see him, he had on a nice-looking suit and tie. Mrs. Powers never combed her hair or changed her dress. It was always dirty, loose and sloppy. She gave Mama lots of advice and kept her posted on everything that occurred in the neighborhood. Mama never had to sit up to see what time any of her kids got home at night. Mrs. Powers did it for her.

Mama was nice to Mrs. Powers, as she was to everyone. She rode to town with Will and Mrs. Powers once, which was enough. Mama came home laughing about how Mrs. Powers told Will how to drive. Mrs. Powers couldn't drive, but she constantly said to Will, "Now be careful, Will. You see all those fools running around out there?"

From then on Mama used that as a joke. When I drove too fast she'd say, "Now, Billie, you see all those fools running around out there?" That meant slow down and we'd both laugh. Mama even said it after we came back to Nebraska—and I use it on my husband now since I can't drive due to poor eyesight.

Chapter Eight

SCHOOL STARTS

Salem to us was a big city. The population in 1920 was 17,679; in 1930 the population was 26,266.

Even with all the fun we were having, I was anxious for school to start. From the time Nellie came home during her vacations from high school in Maxwell, Nebraska, I could hardly wait to get to high school. Nellie had told me how the girls played basketball. To me, going to high school meant playing basketball.

It was a big disappointment to me to learn we wouldn't be going to high school, only junior high. In Salem the seventh, eight, and ninth grades made up junior high. We wouldn't be in high school until we entered the tenth grade. I was happier when I learned that Parish Junior High had a girls' basketball team. I knew I would be a great basketball player since I was stronger than most girls and even some boys.

I was eager to get to my first gym period. We had to take a physical given by the gym instructors. A girl had to be in good physical condition to be in a gym class. The only part of the physical I remember was that one of the instructors had me stand on a piece of paper. With a pencil, she drew around my foot. When I stepped off the paper she took a look at it and said, "You have flat feet. You'll have to go into a corrective gym class."

I felt as though she had hit me in the stomach with a fence post. All that year I spent gym period sitting on a bench picking up marbles with my toes.

The following year when I went over to the high school, I again had to take a physical. This time I passed, but I had lost interest in basketball. I was now in ballet classes and learning to point the toes that picked up marbles.

I did learn, though, that the girls who were having their monthly period could not take part in gym at that time. It was called "off the floor." As the teacher called the roll, you answered, "Off the floor," so you didn't have to go through the embarrassment of telling her why. It's taken me all these years to wonder WHY we had to report off the floor that certain time of each month. You young gals be thankful that times have changed.

This also reminds me of one time back on the ranch. I was a big kid and all wrapped up to go check my muskrat traps. Mama said to me in a hushed tone of voice, "Billie, now remember, don't get your feet wet while you are unwell." (Unwell was Mama's way of referring to that time of the month.) She proceeded to tell me of a girl she knew years ago who got her feet wet at the wrong time of the month and went crazy.

It wasn't very long after that I was checking my traps again. I broke through the ice near the edge of the lake. I only got one foot (my right one) wet, but I got it wet clear up to my knee. I got my leg out of the water as fast as I could and headed for the house on a high run, hoping to get there before I went crazy. There are times I wonder if I made it.

Chapter Nine

DATING

In Oregon, as winter came on, we didn't have snow. We had rain and lots of it. The rain came straight down; there wasn't much wind in Oregon. There were times we missed Nebraska, but we never missed the wind. Oregon-type rain was enjoyable.

The first time Bertie and I got ready to go out at night when it was raining, Dad said, "You're not going out in all of this rain, are you?" Dad never could get used to Bertie and me going out. He used any excuse he could think of to keep us

My first boyfriend Max White. I liked his car (a Studebaker that belonged to his Dad) as much as I liked him.

home at night. Back home, if there was something to go to, he and Mama never thought anything of taking us out on very cold nights with snow on the ground.

One time my boyfriend Max came to see me. I was trying to breakup with him and had told him I didn't want him to come out to the house anymore. He came anyway. I had the chance to slip out the back door as the folks let Max in the front door.

Dad knew where I would hide out. It was in the room Miles and Dad had built on the back of the service station for Miles to sleep in before he went into the Army. The room was not heated and it was the dead of the winter in Salem—which couldn't have been very cold. Max decided to sit and visit a while with the folks.

Soon Dad brought me a coat so I could sure enough out-wait my ex-boy-friend. Dad didn't like Max.

We added raincoats (or "slickers" as we called them in Nebraska) to our wardrobe. Back in Nebraska we wore overshoes, but in Salem we called them galoshes. It was during the Flapper craze and we didn't buckle the over-loops on our galoshes, just left them flapping and felt so much like we belonged. That was the only thing that made me feel like I belonged during my year in junior high. It helped, but didn't do the trick.

Mama made me a very pretty skirt and jacket. It was orange and white and fit so nice. I always felt good the days I wore that outfit. I remember a girl telling me in a very nice way that if she were me, she would wear that outfit every day. I didn't, though, as it had to be starched and ironed—that was a lot of work for Mama.

Miles' clothing worries were over, thank goodness. Poor Miles had a problem while growing up back on the ranch. He grew so fast that the folks bought his overalls (and our long-legged underwear) too long, allowing room to grow. They bought things that way so we would sure enough wear them out before we grew out of them. Miles could roll the pant legs up (in those days we called them Cheyenne Rolls), but when he got too tall, the bottoms of his pants were too far from his heels. Now Miles had grown his entire six-foot-one-inch and could buy his own clothes and buy them to fit.

Billie and Bertie and three friends in front of the service station. It was our hangout.

I felt very self-conscious. I knew I was different, but I didn't know what to do about it.

One girl offered to be friends with me. She asked me to go home with her and stay all night and go to the Oregon State Fair. I asked Mama. She said, "Sure." Back home it was perfectly OK to go home and stay all night with a girlfriend.

Mama had made me wait two years until Bertie was ready to go high school so she would only have to spend four years in town instead of six. I think Mama was afraid I'd get pregnant if she let me go to school in town without her. It turned out Mama didn't know anymore about city ways than I did. I didn't get pregnant, but Mama never knew how close I came just because she allowed me to go home and stay all night with a girl I didn't know.

The day arrived when I was to go home from school with Mary. After supper (dinner) at her house, her folks dropped us off at the fairgrounds and we went in. What a sight! It was so different from any fair I had ever seen. The county fairs at Tryon and Stapleton weren't anything like it.

We had just started looking things over when two very good-looking boys approached us and asked us to go for a ride. Mary seemed to know them and said yes. They took us to their car.

Mary got in the backseat with Squee. I got in the front seat with the driver, a short, dark and handsome kid named Virgil. He drove out of town a short distance and parked.

I don't remember any conversation though there must have been some. I remember Virgil moved over close to me on my side of the seat and I didn't like what he was doing. I tried to hold him off while being nice about it.

I could hear a lot of commotion going on in the backseat. I finally said, "Mary, you won't let this guy hurt me, will you?"

Her reply was, "Take care of yourself. I'm having my own problems back here."

At that point I grabbed both of Virgil's hands, pushed him over under the steering wheel and held him there. He was so mad he was fuming. I still had most of that muscle I'd brought from the ranch and it saved me from getting pregnant.

Virgil told me I would have to walk home.

I told Mary Virgil wouldn't let me ride back to town and asked her if she would walk with me. Squee talked Virgil into letting me ride, but only if I got in the backseat. I didn't let go of Virgil's hands until Squee had the front door of the car open. Squee said for me to get in the backseat with Mary and he would ride in front.

They took us back to town and dropped us off at the fairgrounds. I don't remember any more about the fair or how we got home from there, but I now knew the difference between a "date" and a "pickup." I never told my folks what happened. I did notice a few days later, though, that the place where we were parked was a side road just a few blocks from our Auto Camp.

Mary and I quit being friends. The next day at school I noticed that Virgil was in my study period room. He never spoke to me and I sure avoided making eye contact with him. The second semester of school, Virgil was not in my study hall. I hoped he had forgotten me.

At Parish Junior High there were two front entrances, one for the girls at the north end of the building and the other at the south end of the building for the boys. One morning we arrived at school and the girls' entrance was temporarily closed. The girls had to enter the building through the boys' door. As we girls hurried up the boys' walk, there were eight or ten boys lined up on each side of the entrance. Virgil was one of them. I felt as big as our barn back on the ranch as I walked past Virgil. I heard him say, "There goes the dizziest ##&** so-and-so in school." He hadn't forgotten me.

Since that was 1927 and this is 2003, I wonder if he has forgotten me yet. Of course, as Mama used to say, he is probably dead and gone by now. May God have mercy on his soul.

Chapter Ten

ACROBATICS

I continued to ride the school bus and help around the camp. Dad had taken the big cable out to Oregon—the one I had used as a tightwire back on the ranch when I was practicing to go with the circus. I don't remember asking him to do it, but there it was one day, stretched up between two trees. He may have thought if I spent enough time on the tightwire, I wouldn't get in trouble with the boys.

I worked faithfully on my version of acrobatics. Mama called them "Billie's stunts." I, of course, did these stunts out in the yard where the neighbors could see how good I was.

I'm practicing out on the lawn so the neighbors get a chance to see how good I'm getting.

By now I'm training to go with the Vaudeville Troupe.

The community where we lived was called Hazeville Center. They had a little community building with a built-up stage with a real curtain. (Back home we used a spot on the floor for a stage in our schoolhouse. For a curtain, someone brought a good sheet from home and wire to string it on.)

The first fall we were there, Hazeville put on a talent contest. Anyone could enter. Aunt Alice thought I should do my stunts in the contest. It sounded good to me but I had no idea what to do first or even how to come out from behind the curtain and get on the stage.

I heard of a dancing school in Salem that taught stunts (or acrobatics), as well as other types of dancing. I looked the school up. The teacher was Miss Barnes. I explained to her that I wanted to enter a contest and I might need her help. I had a little money left from picking fruit and I made an appointment for a private lesson.

Miss Barnes had me show her what I could do. She told me I was limber and strong, but I sure was awkward and needed a lot of ballet. She said I must learn to point my toes and use my arms and hands more gracefully. That sounded like a waste of time to me, but I went along with it. She helped me with a routine and showed me how to smoothly go from one stunt to another.

Mama said Miss Barnes was not to design my costume. She had come to watch a few lessons and had seen the skimpy costumes and practice suits the students wore. Mama said Aunt Alice was to design my costume—after all, Hazeville Center was Aunt Alice's community; I was her niece and one of Miss Barnes' costumes would be pretty daring to say the least.

Aunt Alice designed a ducky costume. My stockings were flesh-colored. They came up to my hips. I don't remember how they were held there. There was no such thing as pantyhose in those days. My bloomers were green sateen, very full, but they only came part way down my thigh over the flesh-colored cotton stockings. The blouse was white and plenty spacey with short, puffy sleeves.

A cute little headband with a crosspiece in the center from front to back kept my hair in place. Mama made the costume, all but the stockings. I bought a pair of black ballet slippers from Miss Barnes. She taught me to put rosin on the bottoms to help me grip the floor better with my feet since I couldn't keep from slipping

My first costume designed by Aunt Alice.

when I did front-overs, walk-overs and back-overs. The rosin made it easier to do front-overs, but harder to do the splits. But I managed. I entered the contest and won second prize.

Miss Barnes was new in Salem and just starting her dancing school. I had been told the other teacher in town was old and her dancing was old-fashioned. The four years I was with Miss Barnes I felt I had made the right choice even if she made me cringe and feel like the awkward, dumb, country kid I was. She was fresh out of Chicago and I must have been the first Sandhiller she had known.

She taught in a large ballroom that was being modernized. A new heating system was being installed. In the meantime, there was a big, old-fashioned coal-heating stove at one side of the room. After the contest was over I enrolled in classes to learn ballet, tap and acrobatics. The first class I attended was acrobatics.

When I walked into the hall, Miss Barnes was busy with another class. She saw me and said, "Billie, warm up your back."

I backed up to that nice, hot stove and stood there until she was ready for our class.

She looked at me again and asked if I had warmed up my back. I told her that was what I was doing. She laughed at me (which made me all the more self-conscious) and told me she had meant for me to lie down on the mat and do crawl-ups to make my back bend more easily when I did front-overs.

Miss Barnes knew I would make a good acrobat if she could get me to be more graceful. That would take a lot of ballet.

Chapter Eleven

Working for Miss Barnes

When my money ran out, Miss Barnes offered me a job answering the phone in the office and running errands as a way of paying for my lessons. That meant I would go down to the dancing studio as soon as school let out and stay until nine o'clock. I could take a class in ballet five nights a week, but I would miss the school bus ride home.

I told the folks I was going to take the job and I would walk home. Dad told me to see how much it would cost to ride the bus out. I checked and found there was a Greyhound leaving at the right time.

Tickets were cheaper by the book and Dad gave me just the right amount of money for a book of tickets. I kind of figured he would. I was learning a little bit how to work my dad. Dad kept track of the tickets and each morning when I needed another book of tickets, he handed me the exact amount.

One morning he forgot. I went off to school and knew I would be walking home that night. It sort of pleased me that he forgot.

I walked out of the dance studio that night and headed home. The studio was in the southern part of Salem and we lived two miles north of Salem. I had about a four-mile walk and it was after nine o'clock. There was nothing to be afraid of in those days. I was enjoying the walk and thinking how I would be showing my dad I didn't need to ask him for money.

There was one thing that had me worried. There was a cemetery along the road and I had to walk right next to the cemetery fence. I spent a lot of time talking myself into the fact that it wouldn't bother me. I was doing fine walking past that long cemetery and looking in the opposite direction when a dog jumped out barking at me. I took off running. It shortened my time getting home.

I walked in the house just before ten o'clock. Dad was sitting in his chair. He looked at me and said, "Bill, I plumb forgot to give you money this morning."

I said, "That's alright, Dad."

I took lessons for two more years and he never forgot again.

From then on, my life was at the dancing studio. I still went to school but as soon as school was out, I headed for the studio. I'd forgotten all about basketball. I went on picking up—or trying to pick up—marbles with my toes in gym but in dancing I was learning to point those toes. Toe-pointing will put a good arch in anyone's foot.

Chapter Twelve

Summer Before High School

I found a very good girlfriend in my dancing class. Her name was Josie and she lived in town. Her dad owned a shoe store. Josie was an only child and plenty spoiled. A few times I stayed with her on weekends.

I'll never forget the first movie I went to in Salem that winter with Josie. Talkies had not been out very long and this was my first talkie. It was a western movie and the cows that were in it bawled a lot. For the first time, I got very homesick.

I was also learning about Vaudeville. On weekends there were always stage acts with all types of dancing, singing and comics between the movies . There were many traveling shows. It was a big thing in the late twenties and early thirties.

The most noted traveling show on the West Coast was Fanchon and Marco. I thought *that doesn't look too bad*. I began to plan to travel with Fanchon and Marco. The folks wouldn't let me go with a circus but surely they would let me go with a vaudeville company. All I had to do was work very hard at my dancing and I could still get into show business.

The school year of 1927-1928 ended. The Barbara Barnes Dance Studio gave a dance recital. The recital was about the same time as school was out. There would be no dance lessons during the summer as Miss Barnes had to go back to Chicago to learn more dancing to teach her pupils in the fall. I was featured doing an acrobatic solo in the recital. I wasn't good, but I was the best she had.

Junior High School was out. Dancing school was out. We had all summer to clean cabins and pick fruit. I don't remember what I spent any of my money for this time. I do remember I wanted a checking account. My first ten dollars went in the bank (the same bank where Dad banked) to set up my checking account. What fun to make out checks for $1.00 or less!

One day Dad came home from town and said to me in a stern voice, "Bill, I was in the bank today and they told me you had overdrawn your checking account $1.00." He added, "That is very serious. You could even go to the Pen for that."

I really got shook and was wondering how I was going to get to town and pay that dollar before the Pen found out about it. In a short time Dad laughed and said, "It's OK this time. I paid them the dollar, but you better not start any more checking accounts for a while." Dad had taught his kids to work and now he was going to make them be honest even if he had to scare them to death in the process.

I liked picking berries, especially strawberries, as I could eat all I wanted. It didn't hurt my back to do all that bending over as it does today. We had a carrying crate that held ten strawberry boxes. We picked the boxes full enough to pass inspection, but no fuller, as we were anxious to get started on our next crate. We were paid by the box, not the weight.

Our social life was the Sunday school and the BYPU. I remember a lot of swimming. There was no outdoor swimming pool in Salem but there were wonderful, safe places to swim along the Willamette River. Our first summer was spent picking fruit, going to fun things at the Baptist church and swimming in the Willamette River.

Miles bought a bicycle. I couldn't wait to ride that bike. Miles held it for me while I got on but as soon as he let go of the bike, it fell over. I was used to getting on a horse. When I got my right foot in the stirrup, the horse took off. Not so with a bike. I finally got the hang of it. Whenever Miles wasn't on his bike, I was.

One time Mama called out the door and said, "Billie, get in here. I've got to talk to you." I knew I'd done something very bad.

Mama told me that Aunt Alice had heard that I had ridden the bike out on the road without stockings on. This was, after all, Aunt Alice's community and we must not do anything to tarnish her name. All girls wore dresses in those days and they sure better have stockings on as well.

This reminds me of a second cousin we learned we had but didn't know about until we got to Salem. Her name was Mary and she lived up near Seattle, Washington. Aunt Alice told us about her and we started corresponding. It wasn't long before Mary was coming down to visit us. In her letter saying she was coming, she asked if she should bring her jeans. We didn't know what jeans were but we told her to bring them.

When she arrived, we learned that jeans were girls' long pants. It was a long time before girls would wear shorts.

Soon summer was over and it was time to start back to school. This time it would be real high school but I wasn't interested in school or basketball that year. I was anxious to get back to dancing school.

Billie Snyder left front facing the middle. (Photo courtesy Gunnell & Robb Studio)

Chapter Thirteen

High School

High school offered three courses: college prep, home economics and business. College-prep with all that Latin sounded like Greek to me. I sure didn't want anything to do with cooking. I chose business. The business course had classes in typing, shorthand, spelling, salesmanship, bookkeeping, penmanship and business English. None of them sounded too hard.

After school ended each day I would head for the dancing studio, a distance of about ten blocks through town. A few weeks into ballet and acrobatics, I was getting muscles in the right places. I was able to do my "stunts" with more control and grace. I had one new problem. I was getting fat.

I wouldn't have anything to eat after my lunch at school until I got home about nine-thirty. Then I would stuff myself and top it off with a big chunk of chocolate cake. Finally I asked the folks to hide the cake so I wouldn't be tempted. They did and then I had to spend a lot of time searching for it.

This was back in flapper days. Girls were supposed to be flat-chested or try to make themselves look flat-chested. I had a big problem; I wasn't the least bit flat-chested. The bras then were made to flatten a gal's chest, no cups. I couldn't get a bra that worked. With the muscles I'd built up doing acrobatics and my non-flat chest, I kept breaking out.

I asked Mama to make me a bra out of canvas. It took her several tries, but she finally got it just right. It did the job.

As I remember the years we were in Salem, Bertie was often the family clown. She would pop up with the darndest things that made everyone laugh.

One beautiful morning Bertie and I were outside shaking a pile of throw rugs. Mama was out there, but in back of us. Bertie hollered, "HEY, MAMA, THIS IS BILL DOING A SCARF DANCE!" Bertie was flipping that rug back and forth in front of her as she jumped from side to side. She looked exactly like an awkward bullfighter. Mama laughed. I couldn't laugh. It was too close to the truth.

Along with putting on more weight, I was getting stronger in the right places. I was able to bend further frontward, backward, and sideways. Yes, I was also getting somewhat more graceful. I could now point my toes, making my feet look not so short and stubby. My hands had milked too many cows to ever take on a beautiful ballet pose, but even they looked better.

Miss Barnes put on many dance programs for different causes and I always did the acrobatic solo. To get to do a solo was quite an honor. I soon got used to it.

In the last dance recital before I left to come back to Nebraska with the family, Miss Barnes put me in a line of dancers in toe shoes. I'd come a long way in dancing, but even I could tell my short, fat, stubby legs did not look right sticking out of that fluffy tutu. I don't have a picture of myself on point (as they say now). The reason is: I never kept one.

Billie in her very early dancing days caught in the process of doing a front over.

The last dance recital was given at the same theatre where our graduation ceremony was held the next morning. Dad had seen me practice my "stunts" out on the front lawn, but he never came to see me at the theatre. This hurt my feelings, but I never let on. He did come with Mama to watch Bertie and me walk up on the stage and receive our graduation diplomas.

Bob Payne, our Baptist preacher's son, was in our graduating class along with over two hundred other graduates. After the exercises let out, Preacher Payne and his son Bob were standing out on the sidewalk talking to Mama and Dad. As Bertie and I walked up, Preacher Payne turned to me and asked, "What are you going to do with your life?"

Without waiting for me to answer, he went on in a deeply disgusted tone, "The very idea! You being up on that stage last night with hardly any clothes on."

His son Bob looked up at his father and said in a surprised, sarcastic tone, "OH, so that's where you were last night."

Preacher Payne cut the conversation short and we went our separate ways.

Dad, Mama, Bertie and I headed toward our new car, a Chevrolet. It was a sedan. Each door had a window that you could roll down by turning a little crank just below the glass.

We'd had quite a problem a little less than a year ago. Mama, Bertie and I wanted a new car. Dad kept saying we didn't need a new car, adding that our old

Mama and our new car.

1926 Model T Ford would get us back to Nebraska. One of his arguments was that none of us could drive a gearshift car. (Miles could drive a gearshift car, but he had joined the army and was in the Philippines. He wouldn't be home until the following summer.)

I remembered Dad making the remark years back that if Henry Ford ever quit making the Model T, he would never buy another Ford. He thought he would buy a Buick. A Buick sounded good to me. Our old Ford was so old fashioned, besides looking so tough and plenty used. I figured here was a family problem I could take care of.

Without telling anyone, I looked up the Buick dealer in Salem. The dealer turned out to be a very nice, old man. I told him my story as follows: "We need a new car. We have a 1926 Model T Ford and none of us can drive a gearshift car. Dad once said if Henry ever stopped making the Model T's, he would never buy another Ford. Well, Henry has stopped the Model T's and is doing the Model A, which, of course, is a gearshift."

I told him I once heard Dad say he might buy a Buick, but there was a problem. None of us could drive a gearshift car. But here was my plan: he would teach me to drive real well. Then he'd come out to show Dad a new car. Dad would say, "No one here can drive this thing." Then he was to say, "I'll bet this girl can drive it."

Mr. Wilson thought it sounded like a sure sale. He spent several hours on weekends teaching me to drive. He even took me up in the mountains close to Salem so that I would be comfortable driving on the narrow, twisty, mountain roads.

I let him know a good time to come out and show Dad the car. He came at the appointed time and Dad and Mama agreed to go for a ride. Dad got in the front seat with Mr. Wilson. Mama got in the back and I got in the back with her, just for the ride.

We headed down the road with Mr. Wilson demonstrating his new 1930 Buick. Dad, after having a nice ride, told Mr. Wilson, "I can't buy a new car until my son gets home from the Army next summer." Then he added, "And none of us can drive a gearshift car."

I perked right up saying, "Dad, Max (my boyfriend), showed me how to drive his old stripped-down Maxwell and it's a gearshift."

Mr. Wilson said, "Why not let her try? I'll watch her closely."

Dad unwillingly said, "Alright."

Dad got in the backseat. I got up front and under the steering wheel real fast. I shifted gears and started down the road without any help from Mr. Wilson. In fact, I put on a good show. Even Dad was impressed.

He finally told Mr. Wilson, "Well alright, but I'll have to think it over."

Dad decided if he was going to have to buy a new car, he might as well look'em all over and get the best price possible. Dad could not use the excuse that no one in the family was able to drive a gearshift.

Dad wound up buying a Chevrolet. I surely was hoping for a Buick because it was showier than a Chevrolet. I also felt let down and embarrassed and very sorry for Mr. Wilson. He was a great old guy. He could have turned me over to one of his salesmen whose job it was to teach new drivers to drive. I guess he knew better than to turn a big country kid over to a salesman in a car.

Mr. Wilson must not have been too mad at me. I went in his Buick garage to sell him tickets to our next dance recital. He bought two. He also bought two tickets from me for our dance recital the next spring of 1931.

Bertie and me showing off our new Chevrolet that had glass on all four doors.

Chapter Fourteen

THE SUMMER OF 1930

Bertie and I would graduate from high school in the spring of 1931. In early 1930 Dad decided to sell the Wenatchee Auto Camp and travel during the summer. Mama's mother lived in Long Beach and Mama wanted to visit her. Dad wanted to go over to the Hopi Reservation in Northern Arizona and see their annual Snake Dances.

Miss Barnes had told me of a good acrobatic teacher in Los Angeles. I informed the folks I was going to Los Angeles and take lessons from him. The only problem was that lessons cost $50.00 for a month. I had no idea how I would get fifty dollars to pay for those lessons, but I was going to find a way. All I could think of was a month of acrobatics with that wonderful man teacher.

We were all planning big on that trip to California but we had to sell the auto camp first. The market on Wall Street had crashed the year before. If a person owned a piece of property and wanted to get rid of it, he couldn't sell it. No one had any cash. Time went on and things got pretty scary. It looked like we wouldn't be able to sell the camp. Mostly people just traded places. People who had property that was paid for could still do business.

Dad finally traded the Wenatchee Auto Camp straight across for a house in town. The house wasn't anything to brag about, but it was our first house in town and we thought it was great. We moved all of our stuff into the new home and got ready for our trip to California.

We would be back in time for school to start in the fall. It would be wonderful to live in a house in town until school was out the next spring. After that Miles would be back from his hitch in the Philippines. We would be a family again, ready to head back to Nebraska.

Nellie had married Harry Yost the year before and moved to Maxwell, Nebraska. We were eager to see Nellie again.

During the past year at Miss Barnes' dance studio, I had worked hard at acrobatics. I was trying to get good enough to travel with the Fanchon and Marco Vaudeville Company. I was still working hard on the ballet so I'd be graceful. I had gotten much better. As soon as school was out we headed for Long Beach to see Grandma McCance. I had with me the name and studio address of the great acrobatic teacher.

We traveled much the same way we did from Nebraska to Oregon only this time we had two bedrolls instead of four—one for Dad and Mama, and one for Bertie and me.

The bedrolls rode on the front fenders of our new car. Mama had learned to drive the gearshift, but she let me drive some of the way. We both had to watch out and be sure to use the correct traffic signals. Back before cars had turn lights, the driver had to use his left arm to signal turns.

We drove all the way down and back without drivers' licenses. I know we didn't even think of it. I don't know if we needed them or not. A patrolman never stopped us, so I guess it didn't matter.

I was finally grown up and really felt it. I remember the whole trip as being great. Dad continued with his history stories as we traveled along.

Driving through Los Angeles stands out in my mind. The road, or highway as it is now called, went down the main street of the city. The street was narrow and the buildings were old. We reached Grandma's that evening.

The next day, after getting settled in at Grandma's, I asked the folks if I could just look the teacher up and talk to him. Dad, Mama and I went back to Los Angeles and found the address. I've forgotten the teacher's name, but I'll never forget that address. It was First and Vermont. Mama went in with me. Dad stayed in the car.

After talking to the teacher, Mama gave him $50.00 for a month of lessons. When we got back to the car, Dad asked Mama if she'd paid the teacher and she answered, "Yes."

Dad asked her if she'd given him cash and Mama said, "Yes."

Dad said in a disapproving voice, "I was gonna make him take a check."

Dad and Mama both went with me and watched my first lesson. Later Dad said the instructor told him I'd make a good acrobat and that he could have me in the movies in less than a year. It was so unlike Dad to tell me that. Now I knew I had to find a way to stay in Los Angeles and get in the movies.

Leaving Bertie and me with Grandma, Mama and Dad took their trip to northern Arizona to see the Indian snake dances. I took the electric train from Long Beach to First and Vermont in Los Angeles three times a week for my dancing lesson. Bertie and Grandma were great pals.

Bertie and I had plenty of time to spend on the beach that was only a few blocks from Grandma's. We put on our bathing suits at Grandma's and wore a robe over them as we walked to the beach.

There's a time Bertie and I both remember clearly. We were walking to the beach one hot, breezy day. The breeze felt so good, we let our robes flap open. Suddenly a cop appeared out of nowhere, telling us we had to hold our robes closed until we got down on the beach. Our bathing suits were one piece, with legs that came halfway to our knees. They had a full skirt the same length as the legs. Today we'd feel overdressed going to the beach with that much on.

Before the folks left for Arizona, Mama gave us each $5.00. Then Dad gave us each $5.00. Neither saw the other one give us the money. This had never happened before. Bertie and I held a conference and decided there was really

The type of bathing suits we were wearing when the police almost picked us up for exposure.

no need to tell them of their mistake. We had a good time shopping while the folks were gone.

I had one big worry on my shoulders. How was I going to manage to stay in Los Angeles when the folks headed back to Salem? I still had one year of high school left. When the thought of not graduating with my class hit me, I pushed it away and only thought of being in the movies.

One night I had a dream. Bertie graduated and I wasn't with her. The folks went back to Nebraska and I wasn't with them. I just wasn't anywhere. I woke out of that dream knowing I'd better think over being in the movies some more.

In a short time, I knew I wanted to go back to school and graduate with my class. I also knew I wanted to go back to Nebraska. I wasn't ready to leave my family yet.

I enjoyed riding the electric train from Long Beach to Los Angeles and back. It would be after dark when the train reached Long Beach. I walked the twelve blocks from the train stop to Grandma's after dark. From what I read, a gal couldn't do that now.

I can't find the population figure for Long Beach in 1930. It seemed like a big town to me. I did find on the Internet that Long Beach had an influx of families from Iowa before 1930. Long Beach was referred to as Iowa by the Sea. That might have been the reason it felt safe.

Mama and Dad returned from Arizona. Mama said the snake dances were really something to see. They'd driven many miles out in the desert over clay-packed trails to where the dances were held. As soon as the dances were over, Dad had said, "We'd better head back. If these Indians pray for rain, they'll get it." Sure enough, as they headed west they watched big rain clouds gathering. There was a big rain that night where the Indians danced.

Thirteen years later I was privileged to see the snake dances in the same spot. The only difference was they didn't get rain that time.

Mama wanted more time with her mother. They didn't know it, but it was the last time they would see each other.

Bertie and I spent a lot of time down on the beach. Dad visited with anyone he saw standing around.

One evening Dad was standing talking to a man out on Grandma's lawn. Just as I walked out the door, I heard Dad say, "She practices out here every evening." He told me he was telling this man about the lessons I'd taken in Los Angeles and how I could bend double. That was the first and only time I'd ever heard my dad brag on me. I felt good about that for several days.

There was one more thing Dad wanted to do—drive across the border into Old Mexico so he could go into a bar and have a beer. The United States had been "dry" for almost ten years.

Dad, Mama, Bertie and I drove from Long Beach to Tijuana, Mexico. The first thing we did in Tijuana was to go into a crummy bar (the first bar for Mama, Bertie and me). Dad ordered four glasses of beer. We all sat there slowly drinking our beer—another first for Mama, Bertie and me. Dad was doing a great loud AAAH with every swallow. Bertie, Mama and I just sat there and slowly drank ours, not liking the taste but not wanting to say so. I know I was trying hard not to make a bad face with each swallow.

Dad said there was a lady he wanted to look up in Los Angeles. He had her address since she was the wife of an old cowboy friend of his. Dad had corresponded with him over the years, up until his death a few years back. He'd never met the man's wife.

I don't remember the friend's name. Dad said the man had married a society lady and she was a good golfer. We had heard of golfing and knew that women golfers were an oddity. Dad said he would like to meet the old boy's wife. I think he was curious as to what a society woman golfer was like. I know I was sure curious.

The folks drove me to Los Angeles for my acrobatic lesson. After my lesson, with Mama driving, we started to look for this lady's address. I don't remember having much trouble finding it. It was a beautiful big white house facing a beautiful big golf course.

We parked in her spacious driveway. Dad, Mama, Bertie and I all got out and walked up to her front door.

Dad knocked. A short, muscled lady with a nice face answered the door. She was dressed in tweeds even though it was summer.

Dad explained who we were. Her face lit up and she was so happy to see Dad and, I hope, the rest of us. She asked us in and sat us down in the most comfortable chairs. What stands out most in my mind is that sometime during the afternoon, a lady came in pushing a cart with lots of fruit on it. Back home we only ate at mealtime.

The time came to pack up the new car and head back to Salem for our last winter in Oregon. I don't remember anything exciting happening on the trip back to Salem. What I remember most were all the stands along the side of the road that sold all the orange juice you could drink for a dime.

Bathing suits from the same era.
Left to right: unknown friend, Billie,
Bertie, Odith Huffman and
Opal Huffman

Chapter Fifteen

Last Year of High School

We arrived back in Salem and settled into our new-old house in town. Bertie and I started back to school. I started back to dancing in Miss Barnes's dancing studio.

Things were different that year. Miss Barnes was pleased with my improvement in acrobatics and put me to teaching the acrobatic half-hour of the classes. The dancing classes were an hour each. The first half-hour was acrobatics, the second half-hour was either ballet or tap, depending on what the student signed up for. I was a good acrobatic teacher. I could demonstrate the "stunt" I was teaching.

After teaching acrobatics I participated in the tap and ballet part of the classes. I felt big-time and had almost forgotten and forgiven Miss Barnes for the time she

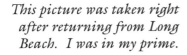

This picture was taken right after returning from Long Beach. I was in my prime.

told me to take a run and leap over a person who was lying on the floor. I had backed up a long way, took a run, and stopped with both feet on the floor just as I reached the person. I bent both knees and jumped over the guy on the floor. Miss Barnes did not even try to hold in her laugh.

Miss Barnes, a tall, skinny, graceful person, showed me how to do a graceful ballet leap with one leg leading. It's a long, beautiful, high leap with your best leg out in front. At the top of the leap, it looks like you are doing the splits in the air.

One of my legs weighed about as much as Miss Barnes did all over. It took two or three years before my fat, short-legged body could do anything that looked like a ballet leap.

I had lost interest in school, but I wanted to graduate. I liked typing. I liked bookkeeping—except the bookkeeping instructor had a bad case of halitosis and he often sat in the seat with the student he was helping. I liked salesmanship; it made sense.

I didn't like Business English. About all I remember of that subject is: Dear Sir and Yours Truly. I barely passed spelling and penmanship. I hated shorthand because it was so boring. We were to hand in many, many sheets of shorthand practice in order to graduate. I don't remember my shorthand teacher's name. I do remember I liked her, I just didn't like the subject she taught. Come graduation time, I was far behind with my practice sheets. I wasn't too worried. I was very busy getting ready for the end of the year dance recital.

The day we were supposed to hand the sheets in, my shorthand teacher called me up to her desk. She told me if I could get her two tickets to the dance recital, she would give me a passing grade. I took that class period and hurried down to the dance studio and rushed back with the tickets she wanted. I graduated with the rest of the class.

Bertie just told me how the big city library in Salem impressed her. We didn't know about libraries until we went to Oregon. Back in the Sandhills at Christmastime, most of the ranchers we knew gave books as gifts. Each year after Christmas the Sandhills would be full of new books. I remember a lot of book exchanging between Dad and Nate Trego. People managed to keep themselves in reading material during the wintertime without a library.

Two of my books that I loved were *Black Beauty* and *The Story Of Live Dolls.* I have *The Story of Live Dolls.* M.A. Donohue and Co. Publishers, Chicago, printed the book in the year 1901. *Being an account by JOSEPHINE SCRIBNER GATES of how, on a certain June morning, all of the dolls in the village of Cloverdale came alive. Copyright 1901 by The Bowen-Merrill Company.* On the front fly leaf in Nellie's handwriting is *A Very Merry Christmas to Billie from Nellie.* Needless to say I prize this book very highly. I checked the current worth of *The Story of Live Dolls* and found it to be around $100.00.

I wish I still had my copy of *Black Beauty.*

Getting back to the Salem library. Bertie was happy to find the library was on her route home from school the winter we lived in town. I, of course, went from school directly to the dancing studio. I knew nothing of the wonderful library. I was too busy with my "stunts" and dancing to do any reading.

Bertie fell in love with the library. She started reading about Alaska and fell in love with Alaska. She says she read everything she could on Alaska and knew she would go there some day and she did—only fifty-four years later (in 1984), Bertie and her husband Glen made a trip up the Alcan Highway. As Bertie talks, you can tell that trip was one of the highlights of her life. She said she had read so much about Alaska that she felt as though she had been there before.

Bertie also checked out and took home all the western books, the Zane Grays and B. M. Bowers and such, for Dad to read. I don't believe Dad was ever in a library but his love and respect for books really showed.

Chapter Sixteen

AFTER GRADUATION

It was the spring of 1931. The Great Depression still had the United States in its grip. Dad had traded our house in town for a farm in North Dakota, sight unseen. The house was occupied and the tenant farmer made his payments faithfully. Dad would have much rather sold the house for cash, but no one had any cash. He felt lucky to find the man in North Dakota who wanted to trade his farm for a house in Salem, Oregon.

Dad, Mama, and Bertie were ready to leave Salem and head back to Nebraska. I wanted to stay in Salem a while longer. I had a boyfriend. I planned to marry the guy. Lowell said he would come to Nebraska and live on a ranch. I worried about taking him up to the ranch. He wasn't ranch material, but I still wasn't ready to tell him goodbye. The comforting thought there was, "Oh well, his mother will never let him come." She didn't.

Miles wasn't due back from the Army for another two weeks. Mama, Dad and Bertie were going up to visit our cousins the Steins who lived eight miles south of Bremerton, Washington, on Puget Sound. Over the years Bertie and Mary Stein (the girl with the jeans) had become good friends.

The folks also planned a trip up to Canada. It was agreed I could stay in Salem while they visited Steins. I'd join them when they were ready to go to Canada.

The last few weeks in dancing school I had been helping six-year-old Pauline Zoë with her acrobatics. Little Pauline wasn't as good at acrobatics as her mother, Mrs. Zoe, thought she was. That didn't matter. I liked Pauline and her mother and they liked me. Mrs. Zoe was a single mother. Single mothers were rare in the 1930s. Mrs. Zoe had a very good job for a woman in those days. She was a linotype operator on the Salem newspaper. She asked me to stay with her and help Pauline with her acrobatics until it was time to join my folks.

Much to my surprise, Mama and Dad agreed to my staying those last few days in Salem. Everything worked out fine. Lowell and I watched Pauline. I helped Pauline with her acrobatics. Mrs. Zoe kept the cookie jar full for Pauline, Lowell and me.

All too soon the day arrived when I had to tell Lowell and Pauline goodbye and join the folks. My transportation to Bremerton was Greyhound Bus (or stage as they called it on the coast). Lowell took me to the stage in the evening. I would arrive in Seattle early the next morning. With all the whistle stops the stage made in those days it took a long time to get where you were going.

The stage ride itself was an exciting experience. As the stage entered Washington State we saw a brightly lit sky over in the northeast. The stage driver announced that a forest fire was causing the bright light. I was so excited. I'd really have a story to tell the folks when I saw them. I didn't get any sleep. I was too busy looking and hoping we would get close enough to the fire to actually see it burning.

The further north we got, the brighter the sky became and then it began to grow less bright and fade away. As daylight came we couldn't even see smoke.

The stage arrived in Seattle early in the morning. I was to catch the ferry from Seattle to Bremerton and the folks would meet me there.

I was looking forward to the ferry ride as we had taken it once before when we came up to visit the Steins. We had taken our car with us on that ferry. The folks had told me I could ride the ferry even if I was afoot.

I liked the feeling I got being out in all that water in such a big boat. A person could get up and walk around. There was a big glassed-in room with many seats so people could go inside if it rained.

I enjoyed the ride, but Mama and Dad weren't there to meet me. I thought that over and decided I'd walk out to Steins'. It was only eight miles. I knew the way as I'd been over the road before. Here was another chance for me to show how independent I was.

I left my suitcase at the ferry office to pick up later. I was a little worried about leaving my suitcase behind. It was a nice new one that Mama and Dad had given me for graduation, but I had no choice.

I realized I was wearing high heels. The only other pair of shoes I had was in my suitcase. They had Cuban heels and I could walk in those all right. Then I remembered I had broken a heel off one shoe and hadn't gotten it repaired yet.

While I was wondering what to do, a scroungy-looking man came up to me and said he was a taxi man and would drive me where I wanted to go. I asked him if he knew where the Steins lived and he said he did. I asked him how much it would cost. Whatever the price was, I thought it was too much. I told him I could walk it.

I opened my suitcase, found my shoes with the broken heel, found a shoe repair shop and had the heel nailed back on. I changed shoes and took my high heels back to the ferry office and put them in my suitcase. The office man put my suitcase behind the counter. I headed off for Steins'. I knew the way.

I headed south on the road that followed the bay. I knew the road leading to the Burley community where my cousins lived turned off that road and I was sure I would recognize it.

Very soon I came to a road that sure looked like the one I should take, but then I decided the turn-off was further down the road. I stayed on the road by the water. Walking along the water was so nice I didn't realize I was walking. I walked and walked. Finally I started to worry about the turn-off. By now the road I was following had curved around part of the bay and I was headed straight north.

I stopped in a business place beside the road and asked them where the turn-off to Burley was. They informed me it was four miles back the way I had just traveled. I walked out and headed back down the same road. I reached the Burley turn-off and now I knew I was headed down the right road.

Not far down the Burley road, a car stopped beside me. It was the same taxi driver. There were two other fellows in the car with him. The driver said he would drive me to my cousins' for nothing.

I was very tired. I hadn't had much sleep on the stage the night before and had already walked ten miles or more. I told him OK, but I wouldn't get in the backseat with that other fellow. The driver said the man in the backseat would get up in front.

The man got in front and I got in the back. It was an old open touring car. We were going down the road when the man who had just gotten in front turned and put his hand on my knee. I told the driver I did not like that.

The driver said, "Oh, he is kind of crazy but he won't do it again." Shortly after that the driver pulled off the paved road into a narrow, rough road with tall trees on both sides. There was only room for a car to drive through.

"Why are you going down this road?" I asked.

He replied, "I'm going to take this guy (indicating the man who had put his hand on my knee) down here a ways and drop him off because he is crazy."

Suddenly I got terribly afraid. I opened my car door and jumped out. I had just thought I was tired after that long walk up the wrong road. When that frightened feeling hit me, all my adrenaline let loose. I was not the least bit tired. I ran very fast all the way back to the highway and headed again towards Burley, "just a hikin'."

I still had plenty of adrenaline left. I knew the taxi driver would not be able to turn his car on that narrow road, but I didn't know how long the road would stay narrow. I was still walking fast from fright when a car with a farmer and his wife stopped and they asked if they could give me a ride. They looked the part, but I was still very leery. I asked them if they knew the Steins. They said they did and they would take me there. I finally got in their backseat and again I was headed toward my cousin's.

Just as we got up pretty good speed, we met Dad and Mama going into Bremerton to meet the afternoon ferry and get me. The folks did not see me in the back of the farmer's car and they kept on going. There was no way the old man driving his car could turn around and catch up with my folks. The farmer drove me to my cousin's place. Mama and Dad drove on in to Bremerton and found out they had missed the boat but they picked up my suitcase and came back.

We finally all got together and sat down at Leola Stein's long dining table to a wonderful supper. My tale of woe got lost in Mary and Bertie's funny story about Uncle Henry leaving them to mind his store that afternoon. Uncle Henry carried several alarm clocks and Bertie and Mary had opened each box and wound the clock in it. They set each alarm to go off at a different time. The alarms all went off while Uncle Henry was tending the store by himself. Uncle Henry was laughing about it, too.

My story didn't shake up everyone like I thought it would. After all, I was there safe and sound. Whatever there was to worry about was over and I had no doubt learned a good lesson.

Chapter Seventeen

TRIP BACK TO NEBRASKA

The morning following my experience getting to Burley, Mama, Dad, Bertie and I left on our trip into Canada. I think this trip was mainly so Dad could have another legal beer like the one he had in Mexico the year before. At least that is the main thing I remember happening on this trip. As soon as we crossed the line into Vancouver, Canada, we learned that beer was only sold in the hotels. We found a hotel, went in and sat in a booth. Dad ordered us each a glass of beer.

I recall how nice it was sitting in this plush lounge drinking a beer. Soon I began feeling funny in my legs and arms and wishing that feeling would go away. I wondered why it was happening.

Mama said, "Darn this beer. It always makes my knees and elbows feel weak." I felt better after I knew it wasn't just me. It also made me think of the summer before drinking beer in Old Mexico and the strange feeling I felt there. For some reason the beer didn't taste as bad as it did the year before.

After driving around Vancouver and looking things over, we took a ferry over to Victory Island. We even took our car again. It was a long ride. I don't remember much about the island except there was lots of water all around it and the land was beautiful with flowers everywhere. The strongest thing in my mind at that time was getting back to Burley where we were to meet Miles.

Miles (2nd from the left) in the Philippines living the life of a gentleman as well as serving his country.

Miles was to land in San Francisco. He shipped his secondhand Indian Motorcycle home on the same ship to ride up to Burley to meet us. He had bought the bike in the Philippines. He was twenty-three years old and it was the first transportation of his own he'd ever had other than a horse. He'd done lots of sightseeing on that bike in the Philippines.

We were eager to see Miles after two years without him. I was also anxious to have a ride on that motorcycle. We were to meet him at a certain street corner at a precise time on a particular morning. We were there waiting for Miles to ride up.

While waiting. I thought about how I had intended to lose a lot of weight before he got back. I knew Bertie had been Miles' favorite sister. She was tall and slender while I was short and stubby. I was chubby before he left and he had let me know he didn't like that. He teased me about being too fat.

Finally Miles came riding up the street on his bike. Everyone was so excited it was hard to wait until he reached us. He rode up, parked his bike and got off.

He hastily shook hands with Mama first, then with Dad, then with Bertie. Our family did not hug or kiss in those days. It just wasn't done. Miles' hand was still quivering as he shook hands with me. He said, "Well, Bill, I see you didn't get any slimmer."

After visiting a while and getting rid of the shakes of excitement, we headed for Nebraska, going back over most of the same trail we had come out on just four years earlier.

Since we only had one car this time, the new Chevy pulled a one-wheel trailer with our camping gear. We started for Yellowstone Park with Bertie getting the first ride on Miles' motorcycle. Mama, Dad and I rode in the car. Mama drove. Dad had kept his word and never learned to drive a gearshift car. I don't remember driving any although I had driven on the way to California and back the summer before.

It finally came my turn to ride behind Miles on his bike. I loved it. It was such a free and open feeling. After my first ride with Miles, he seemed to prefer Bertie riding with him. I didn't ask any questions. Bertie told me just recently that Miles told her I was too heavy and my weight made the little Indian motorcycle hard to handle. We traveled all the way to Yellowstone Park with Bertie riding with Miles most of the time.

Dad was anxious to get back to Yellowstone and camp on the shore of that big lake and fish for days on end. Bertie and I weren't interested in fishing. We wanted to get back to Nebraska and see our friends and tell them all about our life in the city.

The roads were much better than they had been four years before. By now we were used to good roads. We reached the big lake and set up camp in about the same spot we had been in before. For some reason Dad didn't seem as pleased as he had before. We weren't catching many fish and no matter where Dad put our "grub box," the bears found it and always ate our bacon. They sold bacon in Yellowstone, but it was expensive.

We had been there only a few days and nights when Bertie and I were awakened by a loud noise. The bears were in camp again. We heard Dad say in a gruff voice to Mama, "We might as well get out of here. We aren't catching any fish and the damn bears are eating all our grub."

Bertie and I were so happy to hear that.

The next morning we "broke camp" as Dad would say. We left the park as we came in, Bertie riding behind Miles on the bike and me riding in the car with

Mama and Dad. Soon after leaving the park, Miles' motorcycle broke down. We loaded the bike in the trailer with the rest of our stuff and went across Wyoming with Miles driving the car and Mama riding in the backseat with Bertie and me.

We hit the Nebraska border on a hot, very windy day. It didn't matter to Bertie and me. We would soon be home. I looked at Mama. There were tears streaming down her face. I asked her, "What's the matter?"

She said, "The hot, dry wind reminds me of the bad times I had in Nebraska. I had nothing but good times in Oregon."

The Lincoln Highway into North Platte was not the graded, graveled road we had left on four years before. There was a strip of paved road just wide enough for two cars, one going each way. We all felt very happy being back in Nebraska, even though it was hot and windy. Mama was smiling (no more tears) by the time we reached North Platte.

We didn't stop in North Platte. We drove right through to Maxwell, twelve miles east of North Platte. Nellie and her husband Harry Yost were working on the Henry Hartman farm three miles south of the little town of Maxwell. We arrived at the Hartman place late in the evening. We hadn't seen Nellie for over two years. The family, plus a new brother-in-law, was all together for the first time in three years. We all loved Harry. He made us feel so welcome.

Chapter Eighteen

North Platte

Nellie and Harry lived in a large two-story house on the Hartman farm. They wanted us to stay there until we found a house in North Platte. The five-year lease Dad had given the rancher Ed Younkin on our place would not expire until spring. We all needed a place to live until the folks could go back to the ranch.

The country was deep in the Great Depression. Jobs were hard to find. Bertie and I didn't know what we would do, but we were having too much fun to worry about it. We were seeing old friends and making new ones. People did not know us, but knew our folks. They were old-timers.

Many times Bertie and I were introduced as *Bert's girls*. It seemed to be important to be *Bert's girls*. People took notice when told, "These are Bert Snyder's girls."

I remember once being introduced to an older man. The introducer had just said, "This in one of Bert's girls," when Bertie popped up from some place and said, "And here is Bert's other girl."

Bertie and I were just having fun. There were no cow chips to pick up and no fruit to pick. We'd graduated from high school. The folks gave us a lot more rope and we were using it. We traveled around with the folks meeting old friends. We met new people when we weren't traveling with the folks. This lasted a few weeks, then Mama and Dad found a house at 614 East Fourth Street in North Platte that suited our needs. It was a large house that had been divided into two two-bedroom apartments. We needed three bedrooms. We wound up with four bedrooms, two kitchens, two bathrooms and two living rooms.

This turned out just fine. Mama, Dad, Bertie and I slept in the apartment we lived in. Miles slept in one of the bedrooms in the other apartment. We had a spare bedroom for overnight company. Miles and the company even had their own bathroom. We had never lived so lavishly. We felt right uptown and we were—we were only five blocks from Dewey and Fourth, at that time one of the busiest intersections in North Platte. We were near enough downtown for Dad to mosey down to a busy street corner and josh with people he knew. We all enjoyed that winter of 1931 and 1932 living in North Platte.

Miles had his motorcycle and I desperately wanted to learn to ride it. He agreed to teach me.

One Saturday he took me down by the high school where there was plenty of room. He showed me how to start it. (To start a bike in those days you had to keep your left foot on the ground and push hard and quick on a lever on the right side with your right foot. You kept doing that until the motor started, then kicked the kickstand up and gave the motor enough gas with your right hand to be on your way.)

I stopped it and started it a time or two and made a few circles. I figured I knew how to ride a motorcycle. Miles got on the driver's seat. I got on behind him and we went home.

Not long after I learned to ride the bike, Uncle John had his big farm sale. Uncle John lived on a farm three miles east of Maxwell. He had raised his family there. Now all the kids were grown and gone. Uncle John and Aunt Mae were selling out, getting ready to retire and move to town. Our whole family planned to attend Uncle John's sale.

The morning of the sale I decided I did not want to go. I thought it'd be nice to stay home alone, but the folks hadn't been gone very long when I got a dreadful, lonely feeling. I wanted to be with them. I didn't like it there by myself.

I thought of the motorcycle, the only transportation left. It would take some fast hard kicking to get it going since it had been idle for a spell, but I thought I could do it.

I went out to try my luck. It wouldn't start. I decided to wheel it down Fourth Street by hand—maybe I'd get it started or maybe I'd run into someone who could start it for me. By then I was determined to get to Maxwell.

I'd wheel a ways, then try to start it. I told myself if I didn't get it started by the time I reached the edge of town, I'd turn around and wheel it back home.

Since we lived on Fourth Street and Fourth Street is the Lincoln Highway through town, if I got it going, all I had to do was go straight ahead until I got to Maxwell, twelve miles from the edge of North Platte.

About the third or fourth time I stopped to kick the pedal down, it started. I was on my way. It was a great feeling going down the highway alone. That is, it was until the motorcycle slowly came to a stop.

I had no idea what to do so I just stood there by the bike. The traffic in those days was light. It was a while before anyone came by.

The first person along was a man in a truck. He stopped and asked what my trouble was. I told him I didn't know; I'd been breezing right along when the motor quit and the bike slowly rolled to a stop.

It didn't take him long to discover I was out of gas. He had extra gas in his truck and he filled the gas tank. The bike started right up.

Just before I took off the man asked me where I was from. I told him North Platte. The look he gave me stayed with me for years. I was on the motorcycle Miles brought back from the Philippines. It had a Philippine license plate on it. It was also unusual to see a woman riding a motorcycle in those days (seventy-two years ago). I finally figured out the man probably thought I was bumming my way across country by acting like I didn't know what was wrong when my motorcycle ran out of gas.

I headed on to Maxwell, but couldn't forget the look that man gave me. I decided I'd better get through Maxwell without anyone seeing me and get the bike to Miles as soon as I could.

The main street in Maxwell was graveled. I came to the corner to turn north to cross the railroad track. There was no stop sign there and I was in a hurry. I was also going too fast to make the turn. The bike skidded in the gravel and fell over on its side, trapping me down.

As the bike fell, my right hand turned the gas on full force. The motor roared. People from the stores and the bank and the barbershop came out to see what was making so much noise. I don't remember looking any of those people in the face. They lifted the bike off me. I was not hurt. I told them I was going to wheel the bike up to Grandpa Yost's and call my folks and that I didn't need any help.

That was what I did. Miles came into town after me. I had a good time at Uncle John's sale. Miles rode the bike back to North Platte that evening and I never rode the motorcycle again.

Chapter Nineteen

Hospital Work

It was the fall of 1931. Depression was heavy in North Platte. Jobs were very hard to find. I was lucky, though. Mary Frances McCullough, my cousin, was a registered nurse and superintendent of the Platte Valley Hospital. Mary Frances had been a nurse for many years and was a very good, no-nonsense RN. She also had a good business head, thus she was hired to superintend the hospital.

Mary Frances hired girls who had no nursing training and trained them herself. She only hired Catholics or relatives. She had an opening and knew I was looking for work. She asked me if I'd take the job. It sounded good to me.

The work started at seven a.m. and went to seven p.m. with two hours off during the afternoon, seven days a week. The pay was $20.00 a month and three meals a day.

I had been thinking of starting a dance studio using the extra living room in the second apartment Dad had rented. I figured with two hours off in the afternoon I could hurry home, do an hour of teaching, and get back to work on time.

I told Mary Frances I would take the job. She told me to go downtown and buy a couple of white uniforms. I asked her if I wasn't supposed to get a white nurse's cap as well. She said I would have to earn the cap before I could wear it and that would take at least three months. I had to be able to catheterize a patient first.

That was a bit of a disappointment. I wanted to wear a nurse's cap and look important, but I could wait. I went to work—and work it was. Some of it was even worse than picking up cow chips.

The patients were kept in bed, flat on their backs for ten days after a simple appendectomy. If the appendix ruptured before surgery, the patient was kept in bed three weeks. After a ruptured appendectomy, the patient had a little hole in the incision (the incision was several inches long even on the short patients) with a piece of gauze poking out. The dressing over the hole with the gauze sticking out had to be changed daily. The gauze saturated with pus was pulled out and cut off. By the time the gauze was all pulled out, the patient, if he lived that long, was well and ready to go home.

New mothers were kept in bed ten days. The nurse was to see that she did the knee-chest position for twenty minutes twice a day. This was to make her uterus go back into position. The new mother turned on her stomach, pulled her knees up under her chest and lay there for twenty minutes.

It seemed we spent most of our time emptying bedpans. The hospital was a two-story building with one toilet on each floor. We had to carry the bedpan down the hall to the toilet, empty it, rinse the pan out in the sink and take the pan back to the room. We did not have rubber gloves in the good old days. I don't think we would have had time to put them on even if we had had them. I don't remember washing our hands unless they really felt dirty but quite a few of our patients did get well.

The work was hard; the hours were long. I lived with the folks at 614 East Fourth Street. The hospital was at 520 West Fifth Street. I had to be at work by seven o'clock and had thirteen blocks to walk. I remember enjoying the walk in the mornings. We ate breakfast at the hospital at seven, an incentive to be on time.

Mary Frances deeply cared about the welfare of all the patients. You could see the compassion in her face and hear it in her voice. She was also very fair, but if something was not right or if someone was trying to put something over on her, LOOK OUT. Her dark brown eyes snapped and popped as she let the person have it.

I've heard stories of Mary Frances making trips to the County Court House to tell an office holder what she thought of the way he or she was handling some county business. Her sister Doris used to laugh as she told about one of the times Mary Frances got her Irish up. She said she drove Mary Frances to the courthouse and helped her find the office where she was going to straighten things out, but knowing what the visit would be like, would not go into the room. She stood outside, flattened up against the wall. We all got a kick out of Mary Frances and didn't hold her way of dealing with the county against her.

Mary Frances hired a good cook and did not skimp on the groceries she bought. As they used to say on the ranch, she fed good. The patients ate the same as the help did.

As long as one sat at the table and ate, she did not have to go to work. My weight went up to one hundred and fifty pounds the few months I worked there. (I was five-feet one-and-three-quarter inches tall.)

Every Sunday we had fried chicken, mashed potatoes and gravy. For dessert we had homemade ice cream made by the janitor, sweet old Mr. Kemper. I learned a new way to make an ice-cream sundae without all the fancy stuff: get yourself a soup bowl and heap it up with homemade ice cream. Cover the ice cream with lots of honey. Over the honey, sift plenty of grapenuts out of the package. Who needs chocolate, nuts and maraschino cherries?

At two o'clock my two-hour break started. I hurried the fifteen blocks home, changed into my acrobatic togs and taught a class of pre-schoolers an hour of beginning acrobatics. Quickly I changed back into my white starched uniform (a dress). I never did earn the nurse's cap so I didn't have to take time to pin my cap on. After I was dressed, I walked very fast the thirteen blocks back to the hospital to be there by four o'clock. I was never late!

I started answering lights as soon as I got back into the hospital. It seemed everyone needed a bedpan between four o'clock and time for the supper trays to go out.

We did a lot of charting. Every time we emptied a bedpan, we had to go to the patient's chart, write down what was in the bedpan and write what it looked like.

We ate our big supper while the patients ate theirs. After supper we went to the patients' rooms, picked up the trays and carried them back to the kitchen. We gave each patient a long backrub with rubbing alcohol, a treat they really enjoyed. Surgical patients had to lie on their backs and be kept very quiet for several days to let the adhesions grow. We tried to give good backrubs and still get off work by seven o'clock. Many times we didn't make it.

After work, I walked home. Some evenings I had a scheduled hour lesson in acrobatics. I didn't have a piano and couldn't teach tap or ballet yet.

Saturday evenings were special. Bertie and I got all dolled up and went to Jeffers Pavilion hoping we might get a few chances to dance. Bertie's joke at the time was to say, "Hurry up, Bill, let's get over there in time to get a good seat." The only times I remember being very tired at work would be Sundays. Some Sundays seemed like they would never end.

When I got up to 150 pounds, I got so desperate to lose weight, I started thinking of doing something to make myself sick. At home I would take a very hot tub bath, put on a flimsy robe and go out on the porch for as long as I could stand the cold. I was hoping to catch pneumonia. I did this several times and didn't even get the sniffles.

At the hospital the drug cabinet on the wall was never locked. We nurses went to the drug cabinet and measured out the medicine ordered for each patient. I got the bright idea that if I took a handful of those drugs it might make me sick enough that I would lose some weight. I watched my chance and when no one was looking, I went to the drug cabinet and poured pills at random, not paying attention what bottle I took them from. I had a handful of pills and hurried into the kitchen for a glass of water. This was in the evening after I got off work. I was sure it would do the trick. I walked home and went to bed hoping to be sick by morning.

I awakened the next morning and my head felt a little funny, but nothing I couldn't handle. I went to work and worked the day with the funny feeling in my head and ate my three big meals. The following day I was as fine and fat as usual.

Mary Frances wanted me to go ahead and become a nurse, but the only things I enjoyed about nursing were taking the patients their trays at mealtime and getting them ready to go home. It seemed there was so much sadness around a hospital. My teaching business was growing and I decided to quit my job.

Bertie hadn't found work yet. She thought she might like nursing and Mary Frances wanted her to try it. Bertie took my job and made a far better nurse than I ever would have.

The old North Platte Hospital
where I didn't quite earn my nurse's cap.

Chapter Twenty

HORSE IN TOWN

The next seven years I taught dancing, acrobatics, tap, ballet and ballroom in North Platte, a far cry from the excitement of traveling with a circus or joining up with a vaudeville group and being on stage at big theatres all over the country. I was starting to realize life was not the fulfillment of a dream.

The first of May, Dad, Mama and Miles moved back on the ranch. Bertie moved into a nurse's room at the hospital. I had to find a place where I could live and teach dancing.

I finally found two connecting rooms up over Chambers Drug Store on Dewey Street between Fifth and Sixth Streets. The only other tenant was old Judge John Grant who owned the building. There were other rooms up there but they were vacant. The only toilet for that floor was at the end of the hall past all those closed doors. There was a small sink in the lavatory room with a spigot that ran cold water.

In my sleeping room just off my dance studio, I had a small wardrobe for my clothes. I had a three-quarters-width cot. There was no hot water and no bathtub or shower there, but for some reason it didn't seem to be a problem. I had an electric coffeepot. I didn't drink coffee. I used the coffeepot to heat water so I could take what we then called a spit bath. I got along just fine.

I rented a piano and bought an acrobatic mat when I started teaching. Mama, Dad and Miles helped me move in. It was a pretty good feeling. I liked the thought of being on my own and having my own business going. It wasn't until it came time for the folks to walk out for the last time that I realized I was really on my own. It was a scary feeling that I didn't like. I felt the protection I had always counted on was leaving me. It was like a cold wind hit me in the face. I didn't let Mama know about the feeling. As I'm writing this I wonder if she didn't have a feeling of letting go of me that she didn't like either.

The feeling of being alone soon left me. I had enough pupils to keep me in nickel hamburgers with a good thirty-five cent meal at the King Fong once in a while. Times were hard and my students weren't always able to pay on time. I charged my hamburgers and meals until I got paid, then I paid my bills. Life was wonderful or almost.

I would go up to the ranch (home) every time I got the chance and a ride. Sometime during the winter Miles sold his motorcycle and bought a Chevrolet Roadster with a rumble seat—a very neat car in 1932.

When haying started at the ranch, Miles said he wouldn't have the time to use his car much even though it was his "dating" vehicle. He had the folks' car if he needed one. He told me to use his car the rest of the summer. That sounded all right to me. I brought his car back to town. Now I could get up to the ranch more often.

Then I got a bright idea. It sure would be nice to have my own horse down in North Platte.

Dad didn't have an extra horse since they were just getting back into the ranching business and buying the horses they needed. The word got around and a neighbor told me he had an extra horse I could borrow. I asked if the horse was well broke. He told me he was.

I came back to town and located an old barn with hay available only a few blocks from Dewey Street. I made arrangements to keep my horse there.

There was one problem. We didn't have horse trailers in those days. The only way to get a horse from one place to another was to ride him or drive him.

The big day came. I drove the Chevy down to the barn where I would tie up my horse when I got him to town. I caught a ride to the ranch and stayed all night.

The next day the Younkins (who were loaning me the horse) were driving a herd of horses to Stapleton. They thought it would be a good idea for me to ride along with them until the road split. That was fifteen miles or more. They would go on east with their horses and I would cut off and head south to North Platte.

I still hadn't been on my borrowed horse. The horse had been ridden, but it had been some time back. The Younkins were ready to leave. Someone saddled my horse with a saddle I borrowed from Dad. The horse was very nervous and so was I.

I followed along with the two Younkin men and the horses. The horse and I had both calmed down by the time we came to where the roads split, but I had one heck of a time getting that horse to leave the rest of the bunch. I finally got the job done, feeling good that I had made the horse know I was the boss.

The horse and I were going along just fine when I noticed there was a cloud coming up in the west. It kept getting blacker and closer. I could see a big barn off about an eighth of a mile. Something told me I'd better ride over there and I did.

There was no one at home. It started to rain. I rode in the barn to wait for the rain to get over. It also hailed some. As soon as the storm was over, the sun came out and the horse and I were on our way south.

I knew only one family who lived between Tryon and North Platte—the Pophams. They had a large family—among them, two daughters, Sadie and Hazel. We were friends way back when we were kids. We didn't see them often and I hadn't seen them for over five years. Still I planned to stop at Pophams and stay all night. That was the way it was done in those days. If one rode into a rancher's place and it was evening, they knew you expected to stay all night. You didn't call ahead. You just rode in when you got there.

It was late afternoon and I was getting tired. I knew the turnoff to Pophams would be coming up soon. The buildings could be seen from the road. I soon saw their house and the road going up to their place. As I rode up, Sadie and Hazel came out to meet me. Their brother Floyd was in the barn. Floyd came out to take my horse to water him, put him in the barn, unsaddle and unbridle him, and give him a stall with hay in the manger.

I went into the house with the girls. When we last saw each other we were big kids. Now we were young ladies and it was fun getting acquainted again. Supper was soon ready. I remember that meal for the fun we had at the table. There were ten kids in the Popham family. Four had left home by then but six were still there. I remember thinking I had missed something by being from a family of only four kids. Things were lively all evening.

When morning came and breakfast was over, my horse was saddled and ready. I rode out of Pophams thinking that the Sandhills were a great place to be from and a good place to come back to. I began to think maybe this sort of life was better than traveling with a circus or with the Fanchon and Marco Vaudeville Company.

Going was pretty good that morning, the horse was quiet and so was I. I felt rich and happy until I realized that if everyone came at one time and demanded I return everything I had borrowed, I would be left standing by the road in my underwear and a pair of hikers lace hightop boots. My horse was borrowed from Lyle Younkin. My saddle and bridle were borrowed from Dad, my hat borrowed from Mama. I don't remember who I had borrowed my pants and shirt from, but they were not mine.

It was a beautiful, cool morning. I was feeling great until we met a car. My horse left the road for the ditch. He had not seen many, if any, cars in motion before this trip. Each time we met a car, down in the ditch he went. I'd get him back on the road until another car came along. Fortunately there were not many cars on the road between North Platte and Tryon in those days.

By the time we reached the Platte Valley, cars did not make the horse nervous. Things were fine until we reached the long, wooden bridge crossing the North Platte River. The first hoof stepped down on that wood. I could feel the horse grow tense and try to make himself lighter. I got him on the bridge and he just tippy-toed along. I was as tense as the horse, but it looked like we would make it until we met an old rattletrap version of a Ford pickup.

As the rattletrap got closer, my horse whirled and I landed on the bridge railing on my stomach. I was looking right down into the river. I still had the bridle reins in my hand. I got off the bridge railing in a hurry to assess the damage. I wasn't hurt. The horse was on his feet. The pickup was sitting there but I didn't know how to get the horse to pass the pickup.

Years before, Dad told me never to lead a horse past anything that frightened him. He said I must ride him past. I explained to the driver why I couldn't lead the horse by him. We decided if I held the horse tight while he drove the vehicle past us, I wouldn't be leading the horse past him. I held firmly to the reins, keeping the horse as close to the bridge railing as possible while the driver slowly started by us. Just as the rattletrap got even with the horse, the horse sat down on the running board.

We got the horse and car separated. The horse wasn't hurt. I don't think anything could have hurt the pickup. I waited until the rattletrap was completely off the bridge before I got on the horse and we were soon over the bridge.

I was getting anxious to get that horse to the barn I had rented to keep him in. We were on the edge of town and it wasn't far. Cars didn't bother the horse anymore. I figured nothing else could happen when a barking dog jumped from an alley. This unnerved the horse again. I got him quieted and we eased our way on to the old barn. I was never so glad to get off a horse in my life.

I dismounted and gave the horse a long drink of water in the nearby tank. After I exchanged the bridle for a halter, I tied the horse in a stall with hay and oats. I unsaddled him and put the bridle, saddle and saddle blanket in the car I had left at the barn.

There was no parking space in front of my apartment. I could not leave that borrowed saddle, blanket and bridle in the car. It might get stolen. Ever since coming to North Platte I had tried to act like a dignified dancing teacher. In those days a gal didn't want to be seen going down the street carrying tacky-looking riding tack. It did not fit in with my dignity, but I did it and did not get any funny looks. I carried the saddle, blanket, and bridle up twenty-two steps. (Just recently I walked up those same steps empty-handed and thought I'd never reach that last step.)

Early the next morning I carried all my riding gear downstairs and put it in the car. I drove out to the barn to feed and water my horse and take a little ride. The horse was quiet and the morning was beautiful. I wandered out to the edge of town. It was a good idea to have a horse in town after all.

It was still early morning when I drove back into town. When I reached the main street, there was a parking place in front of my door. I only had to carry the gear from the car across the sidewalk. Things were great for several days.

The horse started to act more frisky. He became harder to handle. He wasn't nervous, he just wanted to act up. I told Dad about that. He grinned as he said, "Well, Bill, you're giving him too much oats for the amount of time you're riding him."

The next morning I went down as usual but rode him much further. We were out south of town quite a ways on a graveled road when my hat blew off. It landed in the ditch. I rode down to my hat, got off, picked up my hat and put it on. When I threw my right leg over the horse's rump, I touched him with my toe. The horse made a jump. I hadn't gotten my right foot in the stirrup yet and all I could do was hang on. The horse made some more jumps. (I guess it might be called a mini-buck.) By the time I had to let go, the horse was back on the graveled road. As soon as I left the horse he stopped and stood there.

When I got up, my face was badly skinned and bleeding; my hands were a mess. I was pretty much a mess all over. I'd have been better off if I had let go and landed in the ditch where it was sandy. The horse was not nervous and let me pick up the reins and get back on. I headed for the barn.

By the time I got back to the main street, it was much later than usual. There was no parking place in the block where I lived. I didn't know what to do. No way was I going to go down the street with a dirty, skinned face, carrying a saddle. I was driving round and round the block when I spotted my brother Miles. I was so glad to see him I could have cried. Instead I honked. I told him all my troubles and how I couldn't carry that saddle down the street lookin' like I did.

He just grinned. I parked in the first spot we found and Miles carried the saddle down the street and up to my studio then borrowed his car for an hour or two.

One look at my face in the mirror and I decided I could live in town without a horse and be happy. Miles got in touch with Lyle Younkin and I received word from Lyle to take the horse down to Maxwell and turn him loose in John Toben's pasture.

The next morning I got up early—very early. It was just breaking day when I saddled my horse. I wasn't in a hurry. Dad would have said I just jogged along. I didn't want to give up my horse, but when I got to Toben's pasture, I saw how happy he was to see other horses. I had kept him shut up in a dinky old barn. The only time he was out was the hour or two I rode him each morning and when I took him for his drink of water again in the evening. I couldn't do that to a horse now.

Chapter Twenty-One

LIVING ARANGEMENTS

I continued being on my own, heating bath water in a coffee pot and teaching dancing in my studio until late fall. The weather turned colder and colder. Judge Grant wouldn't give me enough heat. I'd complain and he'd say there'd be more heat, but there wasn't. When it came rent time I had a bright idea. I would get even with the old boy and maybe get more heat.

I went to the bank and bought enough rolls of pennies to pay my rent. I took them out of the wrappers and put them in a tin box. I had the exact amount of money in the box, but he had to count to be sure. He dumped the pennies out on his desk and started. He was not used to counting pennies and it took quite a while. I just sat there. Once he looked up at me and said, "You did this on purpose."

I said, "No, times are tough and that is the only way I can pay my rent this month." He looked at me again and said, "You can't be dishonest and be a grand-daughter of Jeremiah Snyder."

I liked what he had said about my grandfather. I felt guilty about the lie I told him about the pennies. I sat there trying not to let that lie show, but I felt like it was sticking out all over me.

Judge Grant was an old time attorney who had probably gone through some hard times and was tight with his money. He continued to count the pennies, just to make sure I had the right amount. Nellie mentioned Judge Grant in her book

Evil Obsession. He was one of the honest, good guys. When I went to pay my rent, he always wanted me to sit down and talk a while. Once when I was sitting there, he noticed me looking at his dirty windows. He said, "You know I built this building (he told me how many years ago) and those windows have never been washed and they never will be as long as I'm here."

Recently I learned that one of the best-known brothels in North Platte was practically next door to my living quarters and dancing studio. In the six months I lived and taught at that address I never realized that Violet Gosney's Rooms, or whorehouse if you must, was just around the corner at 106 1/2 East 5th Street. My address was 505 1/2 North Dewey Street.

After discovering I was next door to Violet's, I did a little more research on the North Platte brothels. At that time our population was about twelve thousand. I found there were eighteen such places in the little town of North Platte in the year 1934. Many of them were downtown in the upstairs rooms as Violet's were. Most were on Front Street and North Jeffers Street. Violet's was the only house of ill repute on 5th Street.

Other towns called that particular section of town the Red-Light District and people could tell you just where it was located. I was in Scottsbluff and a man told me the Scottsbluff Red Light District used to be on Ninth Avenue. I never heard the term Red Light District used here in North Platte. The only reason I can figure out is because it was scattered all over town and was usually referred to as "all those whorehouses."

I had an experience with one of the madams once. I don't remember her name, but I knew who she was at the time. She brought her beautiful little blond four-year-old girl in to enroll her for private lessons. Private lessons at the time were $1.50 for a half-hour. This was during the depression and not many people could afford private lessons. Most students were doing well to afford one-hour class lessons at seventy-five cents.

I knew this lady could well afford the lessons. In my mind I did four times $1.50. Six dollars a month. Things were looking up. The Madam didn't say anything about paying me. She stayed with the little girl and watched her lesson. She watched each lesson after that, too, but never mentioned paying. I didn't have the nerve to ask her, but I thought she'd surely pay at the beginning of the next month.

I saved the lesson time for her, but she didn't show up and never came back. I realized she was trying to take me and I wasn't going to let her get by with it. Her "place of business" was not far from my studio. I knew which one it was. It was a big two-story corner house on a very nice street.

I walked up there, walked up the steps and in the front door. There was a large entryway with a small counter as in a hotel. The madam was standing behind the counter. Two men stood nearby, but turned their backs as I walked in.

I went up to the counter and told the madam I wanted the money for the dancing lessons. She told me she didn't have it. I hooked my elbow over her counter, leaned on my arm and told her I would just wait until she got it.

She reached in a drawer and came up with six dollars very fast. I took my money and got out of there in a hurry.

Only a month later I saw in the North Platte paper that she died. The first thing that hit my mind when reading her death notice was *it was sure a good thing I didn't wait any longer to collect my money.*

After all the trouble of getting those pennies, Judge Grant did not give me any more heat. I started to look for another place to live and teach. I heard of a two-room deal about like I had. It was located at 608 1/2 Dewey Street—above Hirschfeld's on the corner of Dewey and Sixth Street. I went to take a look.

The building was warm and had the same number of stairs. The small room that housed the toilet was just outside my door. I wouldn't have to go the full length of the hall to go to the "outhouse." I felt I was moving up in the world.

There were three rooms; two for rent and one occupied by Al Hastings, the head of the underworld when North Platte was known as Little Chicago. The room I used as my apartment was next to Al's office. It had a connecting door that was always locked. I knew Al Hastings had something to do with bootlegging, but a lot of people were mixed up in bootlegging in those days. As I got to know Mr. Hastings, I called him Al to his back, but always Mr. Hastings to his face.

Sometimes there would be a lot of noise coming from his room. One time it sounded like he or someone fell out of a chair. I laughed to myself and thought, *They're drinking in there again.*

One night I came home late and the door to his office was open. All was dark and quiet. I looked his home number up in the phone book, called and told him his office door was open. I asked if I should close it. He said yes. He sounded very grateful.

Some days later I got a phone call. It was Al from his office next door. He told me the police had put a ticket on my car for overparking.

I got all shook up, but he told me not to worry about it. He said, "Go down and get the ticket and bring it up and give it to me."

I did—all the time wondering who the heck he thought he was. Little did I know he ran the police department as well as most of North Platte during the 1920s and most of the 1930s. He was who he thought he was! But I didn't know that until much later.

The entrance to the Waltemath Dance Hall was across the hall from my apartment. The dance hall had a piano. (My piano had been repossessed for nonpayment.) My dancing classes had grown. The little rented studio next to my room was not large enough. Mr. Fred Waltemath, my landlord, was a kind old man. He was the father of young Dr. Glen Waltemath whom I had worked with at the hospital. I felt like I knew him since I liked his son. Mr. Waltemath let me have the dance hall for the same rent I paid for the little room. I was all fixed.

I still slept and lived in my room next to Al Hastings' office. Years later when I learned who the real Al Hastings was, I realized that I couldn't have been better protected. If Al liked you, nothing bad happened to you if he could help it. He protected all us law-breakers that he liked. (I had broken the law when I hiked down that long flight of steps and brought my ticket back to Al to be fixed.)

Chapter Twenty-Two

Teaching Dancing

Times were hard during the years I taught dancing in North Platte. People would come to me and ask if I would trade dancing lessons for whatever they had to offer. I traded lessons for milk, which worked out about right since the price of milk was ten cents a quart. In those days, milk was delivered to your front door early each morning in a heavy glass bottle with a round cardboard stopper fitted down in the neck of the bottle. I drank a quart of milk a day because this little girl wanted to take dancing lessons. Each night I rinsed out the bottle and set it back on the front step for the milkman to pick up in the morning as he left my fresh milk.

Elsie Smith was a very good beauty operator. She asked to exchange beauty work for private tap dancing lessons for herself and her younger brother Roy. I spent lots of time in VANITIE BEAUTE SHOPPE getting finger waves, facials and manicures. Elsie and Roy became very good tap dancers for those times.

One day Mrs. Jim Orr from the Parisian Cleaners came to my studio and told me she had three boys in high school and it was time they learned ballroom dancing. Would I trade cleaning for ballroom dancing lessons for her three boys? I had no idea if I could use up that much cleaning, but I had nothing to lose. We made a deal. I was the neatest dresser—or at least I wore the cleanest clothes in town for quite a while.

They were three very good-looking boys, Jim, Burt and Ed. Jim is still a popular citizen of North Platte and until he retired he owned and operated the Parisian Cleaners—the same cleaners his folks owned and operated in the same building. North Platte hasn't changed all that much. Burt moved to California many years ago. Ed passed away a short time back.

I was gone from North Platte for many years, but I have moved back to stay, as many ex-North Platters have done. I had heard that the Orr boys were the best dancers in town. After coming back, I attended a dance and Jim was there. He came over for a dance as I was hoping he would. Boy! Was he smooth! I felt a little pride in my chest knowing I started him out. I was in my early seventies at that time and Jim was in his late sixties. As of today November 12, 2003 I am 91 and Jim is 86. I talked to him on the phone a couple days ago and I think we have each danced our last dance.

Another trade I remember well was with the lady who did my laundry for many years. Her name was Mrs. Toole. Her daughter Georgina was my star pupil. Georgina was small. She was naturally graceful, had a strong body and was very

Georgina Toole

Georgina Toole

Billy Evers (whose folks used to own the Shady Inn) and Georgina Toole, my star pupil.

flexible. She had a sweet smile and was a very good worker, as was her mother, whose business was taking in washing and ironing.

I don't know how I would have made it without this trade. It was wonderful having Georgina's mother pick up my laundry every week and bring it back all washed, starched and ironed. And I don't know what the dancing school would have done without Georgina. She was a good tap dancer and very, very good in acrobatics. I also used her in the ballet skits. Georgina would have made a good gymnast.

Georgina Toole – she was a hard worker and good in all types of dancing.

The twins, Margaret and Marcia Guffy

My very best acrobat. A sweetie named Barbara.

A Very Special Thank You to ...
Befort Photography
for their cooperation in making the photographs from the old Dedmore Studio available for this book.
They are located at:
523 N. Dewey St.
North Platte, NE 69101
1-800-710-8434

Another trade that helped me live high on the hog in those years was one for housecleaning. This most important trade was with Mrs. Draper who played the piano for all the classes that required music, that is, everything but the acrobatics.

Mrs. Draper had a beautiful little four-year-old daughter named Beverly. Beverly took enough private lessons in acrobatics to pay for all the piano playing her mother did for me.

After the Drapers' left town, Signa O'Dean Salto played the piano. Signa had at one time played in an orchestra and was a friend of mine. I paid her seventy cents an hour.

Teaching dancing in a small town was in some ways far different than now. Today's gymnasts make the acrobatics I did and taught look like a toddler just learning to walk. It was pretty good in its heyday, though.

The first half-hour was ballet, fifteen minutes at the ballet bar stretching calves, pointing toes and doing high kicks while trying to keep arms, wrists, and fingers in graceful movements; and fifteen minutes floor work. The class turned from the bar, faced into the room and tried to do all the things they had done at the bar. Now they had to keep both arms graceful. The ballet movement the kids liked the best was the Arabesque.

Teaching dancing meant dealing with kids and mothers. Some kids really wanted to learn to dance and were good at it. Two boys were very good at tap and two girls were great at acrobatics and those four were a joy to teach. No one liked ballet, but they had to do it. Maybe they didn't

Beverly Draper—a little young for the number she is in.

like ballet because I didn't like those ballet exercises. I was probably not a good ballet teacher.

And then there were the students who didn't give a "darn" about learning to dance. These students wouldn't even try in class and never practiced at home. The mothers would no doubt have done a better job of acrobatics or tap than their kids. This did not cause a big problem until recital time in the spring.

It used to be the duty of a dancing or music teacher to present their students in a recital each spring and show the parents and their friends what the kid had accomplished during the year. I began dreading the recital as soon as classes stated in the fall. I didn't realize it at that time, but I didn't have a dramatic mind. I was too practical and down to earth.

I tried to copy Miss Barnes as much as I could in my teaching. There was no way I could dream up the type of recitals she did. That brings to mind the last recital I was in at Miss Barnes Dancing School.

She explained to the whole school that we were going to dance the shipwreck that happened just off the coast of Oregon many, many years ago. Everyone on the ship was drowned, but among the wreckage that washed ashore was an old fashioned oval trunk. The lid was still closed. The Indians who inhabited that part of the West Coast found the trunk and opened it. One thing in that trunk was a smallpox germ. The Indians caught the smallpox and died.

Miss Barnes handed out the parts to the students and to my surprise I got my first solo other than my acrobatic solo. I was to dance the Smallpox Germ Dance. I don't remember too much about my costume other than it had a big skull and crossbones on it. That was so people would sure enough know that I was the germ and was out to kill people.

I was hunkered down in an old trunk. Two husky dancers pulled me on stage. As soon as the trunk stopped moving that was my cue to start my dance. I popped the lid open and slowly started to stand, my elbows were straight out sideways, even with my shoulders. My hands were by my face, my fingers held in the shape of claws. I had a mean look on my face. I used exaggerated steps getting out of the trunk. Then I danced by stomping all over the stage, touching each dancer so he or she would catch the smallpox and die.

When I finished my dance, I got back in the trunk and pulled the lid closed. The two huskies came and pulled me and the trunk off the stage. I then made a quick costume change and got back on stage so I could help with the funeral pyre they'd made for the Indian Princess (who was Miss Barnes) when she died.

I'm on the left and Zelma Luthy in on the right.
(Photo courtesy Gunnell & Robb)

Miss Barnes is the offering. I'm in front, Zelma Luthy in the middle and Bob on the end. He also played the piano for the ballet numbers.
(Photo courtesy Gunnell & Robb)

I learned that giving out parts for the recital is a hard part of teaching. When parts are given out, jealous mothers come to life.

One mother blamed me because her twin daughters hadn't done better and hadn't gotten a better part in the recital. The girls were very pretty and at twelve years of age were graceful, but they weren't interested in improving in any way. I had worked extra hard with them because they would have made a great team in anything they did.

This mother left dress rehearsal (which was always the night before the recital was given) and as she walked out of the theatre with her two girls, she said she wouldn't be back for the recital. I had given the girls a part in a dance line that was mostly costumes and not much dancing, but without the two girls in the line it would not be as good. I didn't sleep very well that night, but she showed up with the girls and things went off without a hitch.

This might be a good place for a comment I once heard and have never been able to forget. I was trying very hard to act the part of a dignified dancing teacher and thought I was getting by with it until I heard Signa's husband Lee say, "You can take a kid out of the country, but you will never get the country out of the kid."

Billie Snyder: Rodeo Queen? Hardly?

Chapter Twenty-Three

COSTUMES

At the time I taught, dancing costumes were as big a worry as the dancing. The costumes helped put the dance numbers over. In a line dance the costumes had to be exactly the same. It was up to me, the teacher, to dream up the costumes. It was up to the mamas to furnish the kids' costumes. It was not as expensive for the mothers who sewed. For those who did not sew, it could be tough. Fortunately, most women with children in those days, sewed. And took pride in her child being in a dance recital.

Since we were in the depth of the depression and I was a practical person and proud of it, I tried to dream up costumes that the kid could wear after the recital.

The number I am most proud of was put on by my beginners tap class, ages five and six. They did a simple dance to the tune of School Days. There were eight kids in that line. Four of them wore little red bib overalls and four wore cute little dresses made by the mothers. The mothers also made shirts to go with the little overalls. Each dancer carried a book wrapped with a strap over his or her shoulder so people would be sure to get the idea these children were school kids just starting to school. There was only one boy in that number. The little girls looked very cute in overalls.

School days, school days, good old golden rule days. These kids didn't have to be good tap dancers. They were cute just being there.

In another dance number, I dressed twelve girls as jockeys. The girls were about twelve years old and close to the same height. They wore bright-colored blouses and knickers and each wore a jockey cap. The only part of the costume they wouldn't be able to wear again were the leggings. They were made of black sateen and made it look like they were wearing boots instead of tap shoes.

I hope these cute kids didn't sound like a herd of stamping horses as they danced. the reason I dressed them as jockeys was so they could wear costumes as street clothes. Money was tight in those days.

When recital time rolled around each year, I had another worry. Some of the kids were forced into dancing classes by their mothers. These kids would go through the motions in class, but would not practice in between classes. At the end of the year they still couldn't dance, but I still had to use them in the recital and figure out something that was mostly costume with no dancing. The boys were my biggest problem here. One year I dressed four boys about ten and eleven years old in Chinese costumes. I had them sit on the floor and act like they were eating rice with chopsticks. What was supposed to sound like Chinese music played in the background. About all that number did was make the mamas happy.

These boys are supposed to be eating with chopsticks. Years later
I spent some time in Japan–this is not the way it was done.

I was always trying to think up something new and different for my kids to do. Georgina was very good at acrobatics. She would have stood on her head all day if she thought I wanted her to. She was also a very good tap dancer. I got the bright idea that it would be different if Georgina could stand on her head and tap dance. She liked the idea. Her dad built a sort of a box affair just the right height. Georgina stood on her head in the bottom of the box and did tap steps on the little board platform her dad built at the top. The platform was just right for her feet to reach.

Georgina got pretty good at tap dancing while standing on her head and she liked practicing her upside down tap dance. For some reason we never put that number out in public. Georgina outgrew her box even though she learned to tap with her knees bent more than usual. I wish I had taken a picture of that get-up.

These poor boys look as self-conscious as they felt.

MORE COSTUMES

We always had a Raggedy Ann and Andy. The kids loved it. They could just flop around doing what they could do in their own way.

*So help me—
I don't
remember
what this
was supposed
to be.*

These cuties were trying to look like Chinese girls.

The Guffy twins Margaret and Marcia. I don't remember the girl in the middle. This stance was supposed to be the bow at the end of the dance.

Sandhills Kid in the City

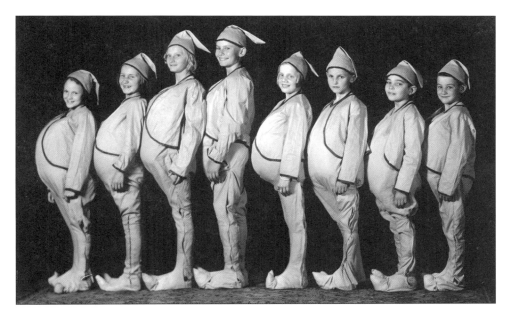

We were trying for a laugh on this one. We got it!

The clown dance. The kids loved this one.

*I don't
remember who
these girls are
or what their
dance was to
represent, but
I'm sure it
was good.*

*Eugene and
Wanda Mae Higbee
doing handstands in
another Raggedy Ann.*

Sandhills Kid in the City

Margaret Steigmeir, Johnny McNelly, Shirlene Foy and George Steigmeir. This dance was presented at the Elks Carnival November 5th by the Billie Lee School of Dance.

These babies were supposed to be dancing snowballs.

What is a dance recital without a wedding? These cuties are
no doubt great grandparents by now.

Chapter Twenty-Four

RECITALS

In the spring of 1938, I'd just finished my spring dance recital. The recital was a one-nighter, as all the others had been. I remember thinking–*This is a lot of trouble and expense to go through for only a one-night stand*. Looking back on it from here, the town could only have stood one of our one-night stands.

These works of art were held at the Fox Theatre and always received good reviews in the *North Platte Telegraph*. Again, as I look back on this, I realize the North Platte paper probably gave me good reviews since some of North Platte's prominent residents had sons and daughters on that stage.

The fact that my five recitals were given at the Fox is a matter of pride to me now. Keith Neville, Nebraska's Ex-Governor, built the beautiful Fox Theatre and opened its doors November 24, 1929.

It was built in the era of fancy theatres, inside and outside. It was also built when Vaudeville troupes made the rounds of theatres and presented their acts of music, dancing, comedy and drama as added attractions with the main movies. This required a large stage with heavy draw curtains. It also required at least two dressing rooms backstage (oftentimes the performer did not have time to run to the dressing room to change his/her costume and made the change in the wings just out of sight of the audience).

This beautiful theatre almost went the way of the North Platte Canteen. The Fox Theatre closed its doors to business in 1980. There was talk of razing the building to make room for a parking lot. At that time it belonged to Keith Neville's four daughters: Mary Nel Sieman, Irene Bystrom, Frances Newberry and Virginia Robertson. The Neville sisters, BLESS THEIR HEARTS, quickly stepped in and offered the beautiful antique building to the Community Theatre Group.

Virginia Robertson, a very active member and actress in the Community Group, gave Patty Birge, a long time theatre supporter, a phone call to ask her what she thought about using the old theatre to give plays.

The Theatre Group at that time were giving their plays in the State Theatre, a very small, old, rundown theater north of the railroad tracks.

Patty quickly called the other members of the board. It took them only two days to return Virginia's phone call accepting the beautiful building, knowing that it would take a lot of money and hard work to restore the building to its original beauty.

While volunteers were doing the work that could be done by volunteers, a committee of three: Jim Seacrest, Pauline Dye and Barbara Rounsborg, started a five-year fund drive to raise $250,000 to pay for the work the hard-working, sweating volunteers couldn't do.

Due to the hard work by the committee, all the money was raised. Jim just told me over the phone from Lincoln that they surpassed their goal by $14,000. The theatre was fully restored to its original beauty.

The building had one thing that couldn't be updated. It was never air-conditioned. Air-conditioning would take $95,000 more.

Another fund drive called CHILL THE NEVILLE was started. Phyllis Swigart chaired this campaign. There were glass jars in the lobby for people to drop in any leftover change they wanted to get rid of, even pennies. Patty Birge told me CHILLING THE NEVILLE took about two years. She remembers spending two *hot* summers in their new playhouse, but with the help of the big spenders and the little spenders, the playhouse people accomplished another impossible task. They CHILLED THE NEVILLE.

In September of 1988 I sat in the beautifully restored Fox Theatre watching Bob Hope singing and talking, his wife Deloris beside him. Bob's eyes roved around the newly redone walls. You could see the pleasure on his face as he told us, "What a beautiful treasure North Platte has in the Fox Theatre." He said he hadn't seen anything like it since his Vaudeville days. I'd be willing to bet that Bob, for the rest of his life, carried a picture in his mind of the Fox Theatre in North Platte, Nebraska.

It was in this same theatre that I presented my last Dance Recital in June of 1938. In a sense, I shared the stage with Bob and Deloris Hope, only fifty years earlier. It was the closest I ever came to making the Big Time.

The Fox Theatre

From THE OLD 101 PRESS:

"They say you can't take it with you, but you can. When you die all the stories in your head go, too."

Billie Thornburg, founder of the Old Hundred and One Press and author of **Bertie and Me** and **Bertie and Me and Miles Too** is dedicated to encouraging people to write the stories of their lives. At age ninety she started The Old Hundred and One Press to publish history as told by those who've lived it.

Write your memories and send them to be included in City and Prairie Bones, a book about the Midwest.

Send your contribution to:

The Old Hundred and One Press
2220 Leota Street
North Platte, NE 69101

www.theold101press.com
Phone: 308-532-1748

Available Now From
The Old Hundred and One Press:

Bertie and Me

Billie Snyder Thornburg's first book. A humorous and historical account of two little girls growing up on a Nebraska Sandhill ranch in the early 1900s.

Bertie and Me and Miles Too

Billie Snyder Thornburg continues telling of early Sandhill life with stories about her brother Miles, home remedies, Model T's, privies and old time roundups.

If Morning Never Comes

by Bill VandenBush. The powerful story of a soldier's near-death experience in Vietnam. "*A priceless gift to anyone in search of their own spiritual path...enormously inspirational.*" – Nora Fitzgerald

Miracle in the Ozarks

by Chester Funkhouser. The touching story of a grandfather's love, a child's belief in miracles, and survival of the human spirit in the face of cancer.

Are We There Yet?

by Lori Clinch. A hilarious look at one woman's experiences raising four sons. Not meant as a parenting guide but definitely encouraging to parents who need to know someone else has kids like theirs.

ORDER FORM
for
Sandhills Kid in the City By Billie Lee Snyder Thornburg
Bertie and Me By Billie Lee Snyder Thornburg
Bertie and Me and Miles Too By Billie Lee Snyder Thornburg
If Morning Never Comes By Bill VandenBush
Are We There Yet? By Lori Clinch
Miracle of the Ozarks By Chester Funkhouser

Telephone orders: 308-532-1748
Email orders: billielee@inebraska.com
Postal orders: The Old Hundred and One Press
2220 Leota Street
North Platte, NE 69101

Please send me _____ *copies of* **Sandhills Kid in the City** *@ $16.95*
Please send me _____ *copies of* **Bertie and Me** *@ $18.95*
Please send me _____ *copies of* **Bertie and Me and Miles Too** *@ $16.95*
Please send me _____ *copies of* **If Morning Never Comes** *@ $14.95*
Please send me _____ *copies of* **Are We There Yet?** *@ $15.95*
Please send me _____ *copies of* **Miracle of the Ozarks** *@ $14.95*
Add $4.00 for shipping and handling

TOTAL ENCLOSED: _____

*Name:*_____

*Address:*_____

City, State, ZIP: _____

Visit our website: www.theold101press.com